The American Jail

Its Development and Growth

The American Jail

Its Development and Growth

J. M. Moynahan
and
Earle K. Stewart

Nelson-Hall nh Chicago

Library of Congress Cataloging in Publication Data

Moynahan, James McCauslin.

   The American jail, its development and growth.
   Bibliography: p.
   Includes index.
   1. Prisons—United States—History. 2. Prisons—United States. I. Stewart,
Earle K., joint author. II. Title.
HV9466.M69   365'.973   79-19372
ISBN O-88229-531-4

Manufactured in the United States of America
10   9   8   7   6   5   4   3   2   1

For
Capt. E. Byron Franz (Retired)
and
Dr. V. A. Leonard
Friends and experts in criminal justice

Contents

Acknowledgments ix

1. Introduction 1
2. Development of the English Jail............. 9
3. Houses of Correction, Workhouses, and Later English Jail Development.............. 17
4. Jails in Colonial America................... 25
5. Walnut Street Jail and the Period of Change 33
6. Nineteenth-Century American Jails 41
7. Jails of the Twentieth Century 67
8. National Jail Census and Contemporary Jails 83
9. Continuing Topics for Consideration 97

Appendix A   New County Prison, Hartford, Connecticut, 1837........... 117

Appendix B   A Brief History of the District of Columbia Jails 123

Appendix C   Police Jails and Village Lockups .. 125

Appendix D   Jail Standards of the National Sheriffs' Association 141

Appendix E   Course Outline: Abnormal Behavior in the Jail 153

Appendix F   Constitution of the Washington State Jailers Association 157

Appendix G   Tables from the National Jail Census, 1970 167

Appendix H   Rules for the Guidance of Inmates
—County Jail 185
Notes 187
Bibliography 195
Index........................ 209

Acknowledgments

A book of this nature would be impossible to assemble without the help of many individuals. We would like to thank LeRoy B. Anderson, Mary H. Oakley and Warren H. Moore of the District of Columbia Department of Corrections, each of whom was helpful in providing some of the general information on confinement as well as specific information on District of Columbia jails.

Richard Carter and W. D. Temple of the Colonial Williamsburg Foundation aided us by supplying information pertaining to the jail at Williamsburg and early Virginia confinement in general. Leo M. Dehnel, U. S. Bureau of Prisons, kindly provided illustrations for inclusion in this book. The several libraries that assisted us in our search for information include Kennedy Library (Eastern Washington State College), Holland Library (Washington State University), Spokane (Washington) City Library, and the Washington State Library. Pamela Murray of Kennedy Library was particularly helpful in securing special books for us. We would also like to thank Floyd Powell and Dennis Paulson, Washington State Jail Inspectors Office, for the assistance they gave us in materials and suggestions. We want to extend our appreciation to Ray Stavig of the Spokane County Sheriff's Office for stimulating our interest and for helping us get involved in the Spokane City-County Jail. It was from this association that the idea of this book first developed.

There is a group that has helped train jailers in the state of Washington. These people were a source of information and inspiration, and we wish to acknowledge their help. They are Paul Collins, Sharon Johnson, E. Byron Franz, Bob Turner, Charles Wolfe, Bob Cooper, and Kathy Briar.

Finally, our special thanks go to two editor-proofreaders, Sarah Keller and Jean Keller; and the two typists who helped us, Sandy Jackson and Carol Calhoun.

1

Introduction

America's interest in crime and its causes, and in its criminal justice system, has been examined in almost every decade of history. However, one aspect of American correctional institutions, the American jail, and its attendant social impact on many features of our society, has been almost universally neglected. The purpose of this book, then, is, not only to trace the origins and development of jails from English beginnings, but also to provide a history of the American jail system, its evolvement in various areas of colonial America, later statehood practices, and local adaptations.

With all the changes that have occurred in its nine-hundred-year English-American history as an official place of confinement, the jail largely continues to serve its original function: the temporary incarceration of persons awaiting further judicial action. The horrors that have been associated with early English and American jails have been recorded many times, but similar conditions exist today in many parts of this country, although alleviated in some jurisdictions. The reports of jail and prison reformists, the activities of numerous humanistic advocates of change, the enactment of legislation to ensure and standardize humane treatment have frequently been of only minor, intermittent, and temporary significance.

The changing concepts in criminal justice have ranged from vengeance through punishment to decriminalization. They have run the gamut from vicious forms of capital punishment, through isolation, to probation and parole. All these have had their influences on the jail system, and which one is paramount has largely remained unsatisfactorily resolved.

While larger political and social units have emerged from earlier societal systems, with the increased complexities of industrialization, urbanism, population growth, and migratory movements, the jail appears to have changed little in its structure, purposes, responsibilities, administration, and control. As a social institution it has largely failed to adapt itself to the enormous changes that are occurring in contemporary society.

The American jail, like its English forebears, in most instances remained and remains a local responsibility, administered by local authority. This local authority reflects local prejudices that are often corrupt. In addition, local jails are usually ill-financed, thus perpetuating all or most of the deficiencies that have characterized the jail since it became an officially designated royal institution in the reign of Henry II. One of the purposes of official designation was to remove it from local nepotism.

Despite the criticism that continues to be directed toward many contemporary jail practices and conditions, it should not be assumed that efforts have not been made, sometimes successfully, according to the standards of the time, to improve them. Many efforts have been directed toward improving the physical conditions of the jails and the treatment of inmates as well as upgrading the qualifications and conduct of jailers.

It is difficult, but necessary and desirable, to maintain a distinction between the historical and traditional concept and function of the jail as a place of temporary and pretrial confinement, and of the prison as a place of confinement after judgment, however the latter might be designated. Not only is there a problem of confused nomenclature, but there is also a substantial question concerning the level of jurisdictional responsibility. The problem arises in the authorization and construction of any jail facility, in its cost, maintenance, and staffing. Additionally, a distinction must be maintained between the nature of the inmates in jails and in prisons. Presently, as in the past, variations are found in the penal codes, the sentencing, the serving of sentences, and in the court systems that involve and relate differently to the jail than to the prison.

As to its functions and its limitations in contemporary America, the jail is presently quite well understood as a part of the criminal justice system. The jail has been the basic stage in the system of incarceration, but its unique position in the overall procedure and in its relationship to the whole has largely been neglected by criminologists and others in the penology field. Until recently even the officials most closely related to the jail have had little or no interest in its evolvement, its problems, and its reform.

Most persons who come into the criminal justice system through arrest are received initially through some facility such as a jail or holding place where they may be confined until they are released on bail or through some other judicial device, or are tried, found guilty, and sentenced. If a prison sentence of at least a year is imposed, the individual moves on to a new stage of the penal system, but if the sentence is shorter, the individual usually remains in what is thought of as the American "jail." It is the history of this institution that is being undertaken here.

In many instances, if not most, the prisoner is in and out of jail several times while proceeding through the judicial system. A person may wait in jail before arraignment, be returned afterward, be held during preliminary hearings, returned again to await trial, and again before and after sentencing to either serve a jail sentence or be sent to another type of prison or holding facility.

Each year between 1.5 and 5.5 million Americans enter, spend time in, and leave the jail. Yet of all the elements in the criminal justice system, the jail, its inmates, and its personnel are the most neglected as a topic of study and examination. Public and professional ignorance and misinformation concerning the whole jail system are widespread. This lack of knowledge and accompanying confusion about jails is not an exclusive feature of our own times. A historical review of jails in England, and to some extent elsewhere in Europe, and not least in America, will reveal the misunderstandings and neglect surrounding them. Confusion concerning the American jail is widespread, and its place and function in the local community are largely ignored even by those who should know more about them.

Much of this is due to the lack of clarity as to what the jail is, arising in some part from the terms that have loosely been used to indicate the distinction between the *jail,* as it has come to be identified, and the *prison,* particularly those prisons at the territorial, state, and national levels. Slang, cant, argot, and imports from several ethnic language sources have not kept identifications of various holding or incarceration facilities distinct. Most of these popular terms inadequately recognize the jail as a specific and unique institution in the criminal justice system which has its specific functions and meets societal needs under selected local conditions of law enforcement both civil and criminal.

The jail, as it is now professionally defined and as it generally functions throughout the United States, is an institution to confine or hold individuals for a limited period of time. The confinement may be while the individual (1) is awaiting trial, (2) is being held for another jurisdiction, (3) is serving a sentence, usually of less than one year, or (4) is awaiting transportation to another facility such as prison, mental hospital, or work-farm. Most jails are administered by local police departments, county sheriffs, or correctional authorities. Only a few jails, such as those in Rhode Island and Delaware, are administered by the state.

In many local American jurisdictions such as the city, county, or parish, the jail also serves some if not all of the functions that have accrued to the state or federal penal institutions. Nevertheless, a great deal of confusion regarding the jail as distinct from the prison continues to affect and plague the public's image of it. The news media, both television and the press, tend to use the terms interchangeably and fail to differentiate between the jail and other correctional facilities that have societal functions beyond those shared with the jail.

The jail is a holding facility of great antiquity. The prison is of relatively recent origin and lately of great expansion. The concept of imprisonment for specified periods of time does not appear until well into the eighteenth century and even then rarely. Earlier and less costly forms of punishment, disposition, and control of violators, such as branding, mutilation, exile, transportation, pillory and stocks, flogging and the galleys, gave way to newer concepts of both theory and practice. The new approaches broadly conceived such practices as long-term confinement involving strict isolation, and forced, but unproductive, labor. Not until the mid-1800s, and in some jurisdictions even later, was capital punishment restricted to fewer than the two hundred or more crimes previously punishable by death. Grisly executions in Great Britain, Europe, North America and elsewhere were carried out by means limited only by imagination.

Occasionally before, but particularly after the American Revolution, reform movements in many social areas were under way. American advocates of change, and there were many, continued to be greatly influenced by the European humanists and rationalists, not just in economics and politics but in the broader functions of social life as well.

The period from about 1790 through the first third of the new century was one of religious and social reform movements and the Jacksonian Democracy of the Common Man. It was a period in which there were legislative changes in criminal codes, in prison construction, and treatment of prisoners. States began to assume responsibilities formerly left to townships and counties, a change that would continue to gain momentum.

Despite the construction of a few state prisons, most American jails continued to serve the dual functions of both jail and prison. They remained as holding places for the wide variety of persons that society said must be kept in custody for one reason or another. For the most part, the physical conditions of nineteenth-century jails remained much as they had been in the preceding hundred years. Attention did begin to be paid to the separation of the sexes, of juveniles, and of the mentally ill. But these reforms were not widespread. Workhouses and houses of correction continued to lose their district identities and functions. The southern states continued and even expanded the county chain gangs that remained a notorious system of misery and exploitation.

Some interest in styles and architectural construction of jails, and particularly of prisons, appeared. Some of these changes were in support of new theories of what was coming to be known as criminal anthropology, which were developing in Europe. In Italy, Raffaele Garofalo in 1885 had just coined the neologism *criminology*. Not for a considerable time would criminology find a home as a subdiscipline of sociology and greater independence in a more interdisciplinary approach in criminal justice.

Both the external and internal administrative jail practices of the past continued with little change or improvement as the nineteenth century ended. A long list of inadequacies can be extended into modern times: housing, food, financing, overcrowding, sanitation, medical attention, cruelty, indifference, nonsegregation. Merely to list these topics cannot indicate the horrors and malfeasance that continued to persist as they had for the two centuries that have passed since worldwide attention was first called to them. Prisoners continued to have no recourse, either administrative, legislative, or judicial, and certainly little to the general public, for the alleviation of jail conditions.

Jail personnel, from the lowest turnkey to the highest official, largely remained untrained, inadequately paid, and without professional standards. Again, there was no public or other support and concern to improve the standards of jail practices and the conduct of the keepers. By contrast, some state prisons were, for the time, model penal institutions, although the same criticisms made of jails largely apply to them also.

It is difficult to suggest why only in the middle third of the twentieth century do reforms long advocated begin to emerge. Perhaps the jails have become so large and so crowded that public attention has been forcibly directed toward them. Perhaps the cost in money has alerted state legislators and county commissioners. Perhaps it is the jailers themselves who perceive their own tasks in new ways and have organized, not only to improve their own relative social and financial positions and welfare, but also to accept new role definitions of their responsibilities to both society and to those over whom they have custody. Perhaps it is the work of the academicians who, with a different perspective from that of earlier students of reform, have advanced more effective arguments based on a more systematic understanding of human behavior. Perhaps it is the young college-trained recruits who come with new knowledge, new objectives, new skills, and a new humanism.

Several indications suggest that long-overdue changes are in the making. First, there is an extended and increasing awareness of the place of the jail in the overall criminal justice system, of which the jail is truly a part. Second, the data on which that awareness is based are more readily available and permit those who are chiefly responsible for an improved jail system to respond. And finally, jail officials are reaching a level of organization, training, and professionalism that will permit and encourage them to take advantage of these developments.

Development of the English Jail

The American jail, like many other elements in the system of criminal justice in the United States, has its origins in England. The essential features of the American jail system were brought almost without change to the earliest British colonies and settlements and were modified only slightly to meet peculiar situations in the colonial arena. It is also necessary to recognize that the continuing British experiences, along with other European developments, would influence American evolvements. French influences are apparent in the lower Mississippi River–basin states, particularly Louisiana. Similarly, the vast southwestern United States from Texas to California inherited Spanish colonial laws and practices.

The jail, like the prison, is a fairly recent societal institution. Probably there have always been places to forcibly confine persons whose behavior violated custom or law or whose actions threatened the security or peace of the group. The phenomenon of confinement appears only as a people evolve from an extended family or tribal system into a social and political system that includes urbanism. As society becomes more complex, and violations of social codes begin to affect both the public and the private, the punishment of serious violators becomes the responsibility of the larger group and not of the person or group whose rights have been trespassed. Written codes emerge, punishments are set, public law is established, systems of criminal justice appear. And jails, however they are defined, also appear.

To define any evolving social institution such as the jail, and to distinguish it from other units of confinement, such as the prison, there is a need to delineate and clarify the functions of each and to assign appropriate terminology.

The jail in the United States appears to remain or to emerge in contemporary times to serve the purposes for which it was intended in twelfth-century England. It continues to be distinct in most instances from its semantic rival, the prison. But it should be noted that in historical, philosophical, political, and social literature the two terms are often interchanged, causing great confusion as to the purposes, identification, and use of each.

Today, and largely on the historical record, the distinction between the prison and the jail is primarily one of jurisdiction. As the medieval political state emerged, political prisoners, war captives, and others were increasingly held in the name of the central authority of the nation. Since these prisoners might be held for long periods of time, and since they were not necessarily violators of local custom or law but rather were serious threats to the peace of the state, their incarceration, retention, or punishment usually lay outside of local jurisdictions.

In addition, major developments were taking place that required attention beyond the local jurisdiction and local ability to deal with them: increases in population, growth of cities and towns, changing modes of livelihood, modification of social classes, and many others. All combined to require new approaches to securing peace and tranquility.

Prisons as we know them today in the United States are facilities that were developed to confine persons serving sentences for a felony, in most instances of a year or more. These sentences are generally served in prisons administered by either a state or the federal government. On the other hand, the jail, no less ancient than other styles of retention, appears to be restricted in use to local situations. The term *jail* is from central or Parisian French and is generally accepted as the correct as well as the current spelling. The term *gaol* (with many variations in spelling) is from Norman

French and is generally considered in the United States as obsolete and archaic, although *gaol* is still encountered in both professional and fictional literature. In England *gaol* is in current use. *Jail,* Latin in origin, has its derivatives in all the modern romance languages. The basic Latin form, *cavea,* can be variously translated as hollow, cage, cavity, coop.

The Athenians and the Romans rarely used confinement (imprisonment) as a legal punishment but rather to ensure either the presence of the accused for trial, or the disposition of the guilty, usually execution. In both of these societies places of confinement appear to have served the same purposes as those of the earliest English jails, particularly as introduced by the Norman French at or shortly after the time of the Conquest.

During the pre-Norman period of English history, the criminal justice system did not usually involve confinement. In the Anglo-Saxon period, which began about the middle of the fifth century, the reaction to criminals and crime was direct and straightforward. The family or kinship group, rather than the state, was considered the injured party. A crime committed against a person thus became an act against the family as a whole. "It was the family that was regarded as having committed the crimes of its members; it was the family that had to atone, or carry out the blood feud."[1] "In time, money payments were fixed as commutations for injury, . . ."[2] We find that feuds occurred between rather than within kinship groups. If, however, a murder occurred within a group, the offender might be ignored or exiled; consequently, there was no feud. There was little need for confinement facilities of any type.

As English society gradually moved through the middle period, the blood feud was replaced by a system of compensations. As the feudal system developed in England, roughly between 700 A.D. and 1066 A.D., the system of *bot, wer,* and *wite* developed. The *bot* was reparation or amends for any sort of damage done. The *wer* or *wergild* was the financial payment made to a family group if a member of that family were either killed or injured. The *wite* was a public fine that was payable to a lord or the king.

Like the blood feud that it came to replace, the *wergild* contained the idea of collective response. The individual's clan became responsible for the offenses of its members and for the collection and payment of the wer.[3] The recipients of the compensations changed from kinship groups to lords and bishops. Compensations became dependent upon a man's feudal rank and the amount of land he owned, rather than the rank of his family. It was during this time that differences were established between private and public wrongs, as well as intentional and unintentional slayings.

During the latter part of the Anglo-Saxon period, the development of the tithing system in each shire (county) took place. The chief law enforcement and judicial officer in each county was the *reeve* (shirereeve or sheriff) who was appointed by the crown. The sheriff was the local government official who represented the king in all local or national matters. He served the crown directly and his job was in part dependent upon the social order found in his shire and the revenues he sent to the king.[4]

Revenues that were rents to the king from his vast royal estates constituted the major source of his income. The sheriff collected these rents, along with other payments and fines assessed by the court. It was at this time that the development of the jail became closely related to the duties of the sheriff and his office.[5] There was a need to confine individuals suspected, not only of transgressions against others, but also of transgressions (nonpayment) against the king.

Enforcement of the laws in the shire was accomplished through the tithing system. The head of a household was responsible, not only for the behavior of his own family, but also for that of other members within his group of ten families.[6] Ten families were grouped into large units known as *hundreds*. These hundreds in the county constituted the major political structure.

During the reign of William the Conqueror, the tithing and shire systems were retained, he added a military rank to the sheriff, thus making this previously civil position even stronger. The sheriff was usually a member of the landowning nobility, and his position was usually for life, often being passed on for several generations from father to son.[7] After 1170, the crown replaced the baronial shrievalty by royal appointment of men of lower rank who were then trained in the royal service.

The *comes stabuli* or constable appeared on the scene sometime early in the Norman period (1066–1285). The constable was hired by the sheriff to aid him in his duties and consequently provided some continuity to the sheriff's law enforcement tasks. In addition to the constable, the *vicecomes,* or traveling judges, were introduced into England in 1072. Upon their introduction, the law enforcement powers of the *comes stabuli* and shirereeve were separated from their judicial powers.[8]

By the end of the eleventh century it was the king who exacted the punishment and tribute that were administered and collected through itinerant judges, sheriffs, constables, and other officers. The king imposed heavy fines on persons and places and, as indicated before, these became important sources of revenue, not only to him, but to his barons and lords as well.[9] The earlier ideas of the damage done to individuals was replaced with the concept of wrong done to the "peace" and the "code of the king."

Because offenders of the law had to be kept secure until they could be tried the next time the king's courts were held in the county, the sheriff was charged with carrying out this responsibility. To meet this need the county "gaol" or jail came into being.[10] In 1166 Henry II through the Assizes of Clarendon required the sheriff of each English county to establish a jail, although there is no record of the date and location of the first of such places of confinement.[11] Robinson confirms this in his writings. He says: "Pollock and Maitland state that one begins to read of prisons in the tenth century as places of detention for persons not yet condemned. 'Henry II had provided for the erection of a gaol in every county; but these gaols were wanted chiefly for the detention of the indicted who had not yet gone to the ordeal.' "[12]

These first jails fulfilled in most instances only one of the two major functions now carried out by jails, that of confining an accused until his trial. We must qualify this by saying that in *most* instances the jail was used for pretrial confinement; in a few cases people were kept in jail after trial. This was the exception rather than the rule, but Korn and McCorkle do indicate that "as early as 1275 the English Statute of Westminster punished the crime of rape with two years imprisonment."[13] It is possible that in rare earlier instances some individuals were confined after they had been found guilty.

Another of the early functions of the jail was that of extorting money from its inmates. People who had been fined were kept in jail until they could pay their fine. They were not incarcerated in lieu of payment but rather until payment was made. Once the money was paid they were free to go.

During the reign of Henry II (1154–89) and under later governments, there emerged a system of law that was new in that it was common to all England and available to all men: the *common law*. The court of common law was the result of a strong centralized government, in which the peasant could now look to the king for justice rather than to his lord. Henry II separated offenses into felonies and misdemeanors. He defined felonies and made all other offenses misdemeanors, saying, "There will be certain offenses against the King's peace such as arson, robbery, murder, false coinage, and crimes of violence. These we deem to be felonious."[14]

At the beginning of the court session in Henry's time and following, the process known as "gaol delivery" took place. In this period the jail procedure cleared all of its prisoners out of confinement and brought them to trial. The prisoners were usually delivered by either the sheriff or one of his designates charged with the responsibility of the jail; this task of delivery was assigned to the sheriff because he had custody over those arrested and suspected of crimes. The prisoners were brought before the judge and either condemned or acquitted at the assize.

Sometimes the prisoners had to wait in jail for months or even years before they were taken to trial. During this wait many died of want or disease because they could not get out on bail. The prisoners in these jails were completely dependent upon their families and friends for their survival. If they had the means, they were well clothed and fed, and if not, they might starve or die from exposure.

Once an individual did go to trial and was found guilty, he was dealt some cruel and grisly punishment. Traitors were often broken on the wheel, whereas common criminals might be hanged or severely mutilated. The penalty for poaching the king's deer in his forest was death or loss of eyesight, and a rapist might be punished by loss of eyesight or castration. The pickpocket might have his hand chopped off. Although the jails were bad, some inmates may have preferred to stay there considering what might be the alternatives.

Many of the early jails were located in pre-existing structures such as towers, cellars, dungeons, and under-bridge abutments. In some cases they consisted of only a single room and in others, multiple rooms. These structures were drafty, cold, and miserable. The death rate was high. No attempt was made to segregate prisoners by sex, age, or seriousness of crime. Men and women, children and hardened offenders, murderers and beggars were all confined together. And all who were confined were dependent upon their families and friends for survival.

In time sheriffs and local magistrates who were in charge of the jails relinquished some of their responsibilities. Thus "the keeping of the jails became a perquisite farmed out to private persons whose only responsibility was the custody of the prisoner and whose only interest was in the profitable return to be made from the fees,"[15] the fees being those charged the inmates.

We see in these early jails the beginnings of the harsh conditions that have prevailed into the twentieth century. There was little concern for the inmates of these first jails. Humanitarian concern was something that would not show itself until the eighteenth and nineteenth centuries. And it would not be considered by all men even in the twentieth century.

The terrible physical conditions found in these facilities of confinement remained virtually unchanged until the sixteenth century. At that time there was a development that had a lasting effect upon jails. A substantial physical change was brought about by the development of the houses of correction and the workhouses.

3

Houses of Correction, Workhouses, and Later English Jail Development

At the beginning of the sixteenth century, indeed from 1363 onward, beggars, idlers, and vagabonds had become a great nuisance in England. Several conditions are thought to have brought this about: "(1) The breakup of the feudal system which did away with the employments of war and service; (2) the growth of large-scale manufactures which rendered employment less stable; (3) the rise of prices brought about by sudden increase in the world's supply of silver, increasing the hardships of the laboring class; (4) the enclosures which drove the people from the land. A fifth reason may be found in the whole system of poor relief which had been woefully lacking in constructiveness."[1]

Because of the great numbers of beggars, and the failure of the harsh measures of flogging, branding, and mutilation under Henry VIII, an attempt was made to control these conditions by use of houses of correction. In 1553 Edward VI gave to the city of London a mansion that Henry VIII had constructed in 1525 for a royal visitor, Charles V, Holy Roman Emperor. The gift was to serve as a penitentiary, a house of corrections for vagabonds and loose women.[2]

As London experimented with the house of correction, the 1575–76 session of Parliament legislated the erection of similar institutions, *bridewells*, in every English county. These bridewells developed into institutions whose aim was to develop good citizenship by industry, religious instruction, and education. Houses of corrections were distinct from the county jails and were controlled by the justices rather than the sheriff. This distinction between the jail and the house of correction would disappear by the eighteenth century, and the justices could assign offenders to either as they chose.

The inhabitants of these early bridewells were the untrained child and the vagrant. It was proposed that these persons be employed in a hospital (the early name given to charitable institutions) and to train those who needed training and to force all to work who were confined.[3] Thus, these institutions served a variety of functions: (1) an industrial school for the young, (2) a place of refuge for the old and infirm, (3) a place for the poor who could not find work elsewhere, and (4) an institution that served to punish and correct the vagrant.

The financial responsibility for the construction of the bridewells was placed in the hands of the county. There was also a provision that an individual might establish and maintain a house of correction out of his own funds. This law providing for private houses of correction was continued until 1597, when another act required that houses of correction be built solely by the counties. Later the private houses were again allowed to develop.

Bridewells fulfilled some of the functions performed by modern prisons, and they should be considered as part of the early penal system of England. They were in reality part jail (at least in a modern sense), since they did incarcerate offenders guilty of minor crimes such as vagrancy (at a future time regulations would change and vagrants would be kept in jails). But it should also be remembered that they existed side by side with the early English jails, which had as their main function the holding of individuals who were awaiting either trial or punishment.

There was some difficulty getting the different English counties to establish the bridewells. Many counties constructed them while others did not, and consequently certain counties complained to the government that they were getting an overflow of vagrants and children from the other counties. The English government eventually threatened to fine counties that did not construct bridewells.

The Book of Orders of 1630–31 required that a house of correction should be built next to the common jail. The bridewells then took on more and more the character of institutions for the punishment of vagrants. Exceptions to this were the houses of correction that were established by private funds, and these tended to retain many of the characteristics of the early bridewell.[4]

The 1575–76 statute that called for a house of correction in each county also provided that stocks of raw materials be placed in towns and cities for use by the inmates of the houses of correction. These materials could be made up into finished products and turned over to the municipal or parish officials, and those who worked on them could be paid. Since many of the materials were, through neglect, lost or stolen, work-places or workhouses were finally established. Sometimes the workhouses were part of the houses of correction, and in other instances they were not. The workhouses were not part of the penal system but were rather established to provide jobs for those able and willing to work.

The English jails remained pretty much the same with little change from the tenth to the seventeenth century. They were bad places to be confined in and unpleasant to visit. They did get bigger during this time and were capable of holding more people. Although they were known as the "king's gaols" they were generally built by the counties and municipalities at their own expense. Once the structures were built, the counties and municipalities had little or no financial responsibility for their operation and maintenance. The prisoners were still charged with supporting themselves.

The sheriff was in charge of the jails, at least nominally. He was an appointee of the crown in most areas, but was elected in some cities by the municipal corporation. In some municipalities, the bailiff acted as the sheriff, and was in charge of the jail. Most jails were turned over to a keeper who had charge of them for life.[5]

Since the keeper was not given a salary, he made his living through a system of fees charged to the prisoners. He sold items such as food and clothing to the inmates, and he was also able to secure additional revenues by forcing the inmates to hire out for manual labor. The jailer charged the inmates for their keep, forced them to work, and even charged them for the privilege of being locked up!

E. M. Leonard comments on and describes the conditions in the English jails of this period.

> The prisoners of the sixteenth century must have suffered great hardships. No adequate means seem to have existed for their maintenance. Their friends supported them, and under certain regulations they were allowed to beg. Several statutes made in the reign of Elizabeth provided partially for their support as part of the relief of the poor. By the statute of 1601, prisoners were to be relieved by a county rate. The County Treasurer, who was responsible for the relief of soldiers and hospitals, also disbursed a part of the funds to them, and every county was bound to pay at least twenty shillings a year to the prisoners of the King's Bench and Marshalsea. Still the help given was very small; up to 1650 the allowance granted to the poor in the Norfolk prison was only a penny a day, and this sum could barely have sufficed to keep them alive. In Devonshire their allowance was increased in 1608 because "divers of them of late have perished through want." We must remember that incarceration in these prisons was the fate of debtors. Charitable people tried to help these people, and bequests were often made for the purpose of granting them some assistance. Thus in the reign of Charles I, George White of Bristol left a gift of five pounds a year to be used for the purpose of freeing or relieving some of the prisoners in the Bristol Newgate, and there are many other bequests of the same kind. Still the amount of these legacies was wholly insufficient for the need. Certainly neither the legislators nor the administrators of the reigns of the earlier Stuarts made the criminal poor more comfortable than the unfortunate poor. If we realize the condition of the prisoners of this time, we can understand why Houses of Correction were regarded as charitable foundations. We can also see how it was that whipping and stocking were so frequently inflicted and that they were comparatively merciful punishments.[6]

There were provisions in the law for the inspection of the jails. These inspections were to be carried out by means of a grand jury that could make its findings known to the Court of Quarter Sessions. It was an inadequate method of supervision and therefore ineffective.

In the seventeenth and eighteenth centuries, there began to develop some concern over the conditions found in the English jails. The first report on jail conditions was published by a former inmate in 1618. Although the report may have received some attention, it was not until the beginning of the 1700s that a committee was delegated the responsibility of investigating jail conditions. A Committee of the Society for Promoting Christian Knowledge, under the chairmanship of a physician, Dr. Bray, visited several jails. In 1702 this committee submitted a report entitled, "An Essay Towards the Reformation of Newgate and Other Prisons in and About London."[7] Max Grunhut has provided a summary of the criticisms of this 1702 report: "This Essay makes six 'vices and immoralities' responsible for the desperate state of contemporary prison conditions: personal lewdness of the keepers, their confederacy with prisoners, the unlimited use of spirits, swearing and gambling, corruption of new-comers by old criminals, neglect of all religious worship."[8]

One problem the report did not attack was the unsupervised private operation of jails. The committee did, however, make several far-reaching suggestions for jail improvement. It suggested that—

1. work programs be instituted.
2. separate confinement be developed.
3. liquor be prohibited.
4. the fee-taking system by keepers be eliminated.
5. habitual prisoners be required to furnish a financial bond upon release.
6. inmates have immediate employment upon release.
7. the names of well-behaved prisoners be published (in hopes that sympathetic persons would help them on their release).[9]

However, the report and recommendations of this committee and those after it had little effect upon the confinement facilities of England. Jail conditions remained largely unchanged, and it was not until the latter part of the eighteenth century that some reforms began to appear.

It was into this setting that the impact of John Howard's work came. Howard (1726–90) was a sheriff of Bedford County who turned jail critic and reformer. He revealed to the world in the latter part of the eighteenth century the conditions of English jails.[10] In fact, Howard spent many of his remaining years, after stepping down as sheriff, traveling through most European countries examining their confinement facilities.

At the time Howard was pressing for reform in England, the functions of jails were beginning to change. They began to be used as places for long-term confinement. They were in fact being used as prisons, that is, prisons as we know them today, even though the early jails were completely unsuited for this type of confinement.

This custodial function came as a reaction to the bloodletting and severity of treatment of the convicted. There were over two hundred capital offenses in England at that time, for which severe mutilations were inflicted as punishment. Judges and juries tended to set free those charged rather than subject them to these terrible sanctions. There were still many people mutilated and put to death, but the trend was away from this. Imprisonment became a favored alternative. The development of prisons will be reviewed in a later chapter.

The jails of Howard's time were not all physically secure, and the prisoners often had to be shackled at night to guarantee their presence the next day. Howard urged that the jails should be both secure and also sanitary. The jails of his day were very unsanitary. All classes of prisoners were confined together in facilities that had open sewers running through them.

A major disease problem developed during this time. Commonly called jail fever, it is known to have been typhus, carried by the large number of rats and fleas found in the jails. The prisoners were not the only ones who died from this disease; jailers also were stricken and the disease spread to nearby towns and villages. (Ironically, it was this disease from which reformer John Howard died.) Present at the Court of Cambridge in 1522 were many of the knights and gentlemen who there contracted jail fever. Many perished at Exeter in 1586 and at Taunton in 1730. The lord mayor of London, two of his judges, some aldermen, many lawyers, the undersheriff, and a number of spectators died of jail fever.[11]

Because of the unhealthy physical and mental conditions he found in most jails, John Howard pushed for many reforms. He urged supervision of the prisoners so as to prevent physical and moral corruption. He wanted useful work and religious instruction for those confined. In addition, he thought that the jailers should be paid rather than be dependent on the extortion of fees from prisoners.

Jeremy Bentham (1748–1832), another advocate of prison and penal reform, pressed for the construction of cellular jails. Statutes for the building of new jails were enacted in 1774, but unfortunately, the enforcement of these statutes rested with the justices in each county. And since their opinions varied from locality to locality, there were few cellular jails built.[12]

Bentham also proposed to Parliament a site for the first English penitentiary, and in 1794 a location was procured at Millbank in London. In 1816 construction was started. Bentham's efforts, as well as those of Sir Robert Peel, home secretary in the British government, helped in jail reform and aided in the construction of the English prison system.

Peel reduced and consolidated the capital statutes and abolished the "benefit of clergy" laws. "His Gaol Act of 1823 became the foundation of the English prison system. The justices were now required to govern the prisons according to prescribed principles. The jailer became their paid servant, the jails had to be inspected and reports were mandatory to the Home Secretary. The graver abuses were discontinued and Howard's suggestions were put in force with the exception of his proposal for a separate cell system. Instead inmates were classified into groups for employment."[13]

Returning to our look at the houses of correction, we find that, after the English Civil War (during the 1640s), the unemployed were not provided with work. They filled the houses of correction, which became more and more like the common jails, and the workhouses, which were more like almshouses or houses for the poor.

With a continued demand for labor in the British colonies, the common jails were emptied of their inmates, who were shipped overseas to many places including Virginia and the West Indies. When inmates could no longer be sent to the rebelling mainland colonies, a new problem arose: what to do with them in the overcrowded jails.

To alleviate this problem, ship hulks were put into use in 1776 as a temporary measure that actually continued until 1858. The hulks were old, unusable, and abandoned military transport ships anchored in the various rivers and harbors in Great Britain. These ships supplied no segregation, so that young and old, male and female, hardened criminal and criminal neophyte, the mentally healthy and mentally ill were all confined together. Degrading labor ashore and brutal treatment on board tended to corrupt both inmate and master alike. The dreaded jail fever was rampant in these unhealthy facilities and was transmitted from one to another on board as well as to inhabitants in the surrounding communities. The hulks were a most despicable chapter in the history of confinement.

Let us now turn our attention to the American colonial period and early jails in the United States.

4

Jails in Colonial America

The British settlers who came to America brought with them three basic English institutions, one of which was the common jail found throughout England. This was generally used to hold those awaiting trial or disposition after trial. Jails had at various times also been used to hold people while an attempt was made to extract money from them. In the jails were confined convicted rapists, soldiers taken prisoner, heretics, and members of the clergy.

The colonials were also familiar with the houses of correction, or bridewells, used primarily to confine the old and sick, the displaced child, and the vagrant. They provided work, religious instruction, and education for the inmates. This had been England's primary response to the problems of the vagrant, beggar, and pauper.

The third institution was the workhouse, which provided work for the unemployed adult and gave industrial training to the young. The workhouse, while not part of the criminal justice system, was a response to the problems of the unemployed and the child in need of training or a home.

There was little or no crime among the earliest arrivals in the New World. But as villages and communities became more populous, crime also increased, and by 1690 it was a major problem in some areas. However, crime in American communities was not as widespread nor the penalties as severe as in English towns of the same size.[1]

Drawing upon their English heritage, the settlers built jails as their first penal institutions.[2] Each of the colonial areas had a slightly different historical development with regard to these facilities.[3] Jails were generally under the care of the sheriff, or as in England under one of his appointed staff. In time municipal jails were developed under the control of community law enforcement officers.

Each of the villages had a variety of penalties for the criminal or moral delinquent. "Fines, whippings, and restitution of stolen goods, often two- or three-fold, constituted the more usual punishments."[4] Stocks and pillories were also used but not as frequently as commonly thought. They were not used in New York, for example, until 1690. Stocks, pillories, whipping posts, and dunking stools were often located next to the jail so that once a person was found guilty he could receive his punishment without delay.

Stocks were generally used to confine petty offenders. The offender sat on a bench with his ankles and sometimes his wrists thrust through holes in a moveable board. He would be held for several hours during which time townspeople might heap verbal abuse or even garbage on him. The practice lasted through the early part of the nineteenth century in both England and America. In the Southern colonies stocks were employed more for punishing slaves than freeholders.

The pillory was a wooden post and frame mounted on a platform raised several feet above the ground. The guilty one stood behind it with his hands and head thrust through holes in the frame and secured there. It was used in England in the 1200s for "forestallers and regrators, users of deceitful weights, perjurers and forgers." Provisions for its use were generally in effect in the United States until 1839 and it still existed in the statutes of Delaware until 1905.

Whipping posts date back to early England. In the thirty-ninth year of Elizabeth I a new act required that the offender be stripped to the waist and bound to a post. The whipping post was a substitute for being strapped to a cart and whipped. It was often combined with stocks and had iron clasps for the hands. Men and women both were flogged; offenders included "sellers of damaged goods and lunatics." Whipping was generally abolished by the nineteenth century, but it was continued in some areas of the United States until much later.

The dunking stool also served as punishment for lesser offenses. It was a chair on the end of a long lever. The violator was strapped in the chair and the chair moved over the stream or pond. The individual was then dunked into the water for varying numbers and lengths of time by an operator on the shore. Crowds gathered to jeer and taunt the victim.

The stocks, pillories, whipping post, and dunking stool, originating as they did in England, were used in the colonies as well, usually in lieu of confinement in jail or some more excessive punishment. In many cases, if the same offense committed then was committed today the perpetrator would serve only a jail sentence.

Two general practices emerge from colonial times. First, the most direct and least expensive punishment was the one to be used. Second, punishment was more humane than in Europe, especially in the use of the death penalty for trivial offenses. Rather than pass such harsh sentences many English and colonial judges sentenced criminals to expulsion instead or simply let them go. Nevertheless, early dealings with criminals in the colonies were haphazard. Imprisonment as a punishment was unusual. It cost less to fine or flog, and consequently these measures were more frequently used. As in England, the main function of the jail was to hold people who had been arrested and were awaiting trial. Construction of early jails was financed by the local residents. Due to a lack of money and concern, many of these buildings were constantly in need of repairs. Consequently, they were not escape-proof, and in many of them a prisoner could escape by hurling himself against a flimsy door!

Carl Bridenbaugh, in *Cities in the Wilderness: Urban Life in America, 1625–1742*, makes some interesting observations on the development of jails in colonial America.[5] In 1640 in Newport, Rhode Island, criminals were held in the house of Sergeant Bull. Sometime before 1648 a jail was built for the use of the entire colony. In 1655 an order of the General Assembly directed the town to build a new place of confinement at a cost of #80. Of this money, one quarter of the expense was to be paid by Portsmouth, which was to share the use of the building. At New Amsterdam the Dutch

West India Company built a tavern in 1642, called the Stadt Huys City Hall, which served as a place of confinement until the completion of the city hall in 1700. William Clayton built a "cage" in Philadelphia for the confinement of minor criminals. This took place shortly after the Pennsylvania Assembly in 1683 required that each county build a house of correction. There appeared, however, to be little progress in the seventeenth century toward providing adequate jails for the villages.

A new Philadelphia prison, actually a jail, was ordered built by the Pennsylvania Assembly in 1718 and completed in 1722. This structure was a two-story stone building with two connecting wings and a yard, all enclosed by a high wall, and was the only facility of the time which made any attempt to segregate the inmates. One of the buildings was used for debtors while the other had cells reserved for criminals. The jailer, William Biddle, charged twopence a day for food furnished to the inmates. Even though the facility was strongly built, there were at least fifteen escapes between 1729 and 1732.

In Boston an old confinement facility was so ill kept that four men escaped from it in 1723 and seven in 1726. The number seems small, but these jails never held great numbers of people as do our contemporary jails. A new jail was built in Boston and opened in 1732, but in May of that year four enterprising inmates jumped out of the building after cutting off the bars of the upper windows. Before escaping in 1737, a convicted murderer, James Barnes, wrote, "acquainting the keeper of the prison that he had made his escape about twelve o'clock, that he was in a very great hurry, and could not stay to pay his fees, but would do it the next time he came there." To relieve some of the pressure in the facility, the Suffolk County Court erected a house of correction which was to be used to confine unruly servants and minor offenders.

Criminals and debtors alike were lodged in the basement of city hall in eighteenth century New York. Because of jail breaks in 1724 and 1725, two additional watchmen were hired to watch inmates. In 1727 four more guards were hired. The jail was made stronger in 1730, and the watchmen were fired. In 1735 the city completed an almshouse that was used as a house of correction and a workhouse for such individuals as trespassers, rogues, vagabonds, beggars, servants running away or otherwise misbehaving, and poor people refusing to work. This is, of course, a prime example of the loss of distinction between the workhouse and house of correction.

Although these early jails were in extremely poor condition, they were better than those found in England at the same time. Fewer prisoners perished in the facilities, and one did not find the filth or brutal conditions in the New World that were so prevalent in the Old World. Their primary defect was inefficiency rather than cruelty.

> Eighteenth-Century jails in fact closely resembled the household in structure and routine. They lacked a distinct architecture and special procedures. When the Virginia burgess required that the county prison be "good, strong, and substantial," and explicitly recommended that they follow "after the form of Virginia housing," results were in keeping with these directions. The doors were perhaps somewhat sturdier, the locks slightly more impressive, but the general design of the jail was the same as for an ordinary residence. True to the household model, the keeper and his family resided in the jail, occupying one of its rooms; the prisoners lived several together in the others, with little to differentiate the keeper's quarters from their own. They wore no special clothing or uniforms and usually neither cuffs nor chains restrained their movements. They walked—not marched—about the jail. The workhouse model was so irrelevant that nowhere were they required to perform the slightest labor."[6]

A good example of one of the earliest American jails still standing is the one found at Williamsburg, Virginia.[7] Originally erected in 1703-1704 by Henry Cary, it has had several additions over the years. It was restored earlier this century and is available for public tour.[8] This jail looks very much like the ordinary seventeenth-century Virginia house. It is sturdier than most, having large timbers in the walls as well as being "underlaid with timbers underground to the foundations to prevent undermining." In 1711 an addition was made to accommodate debtors. Early colonial inmates could receive a form of work-release and bond. The Williamsburg jail is distinctive in at least three additional ways. First, it separated men and women. Second, there was a separation of the more serious offenders from the less serious ones. Third, it had inside toilet facilities (each cell had a wooden trough that emptied into a cesspool).[9]

People were held in the Williamsburg jail until the "Quarter Sessions and General Gaol Delivery," when they were taken to court to have their cases heard before the proper authorities. It was often a great relief just to be taken out of jail, even for trial.

Most early jails were not good places in which to be confined. Often the jails consisted of only a single room, which may have held all of the prisoners, as many as twenty or thirty people. As with the English jails, there was no attempt at segregation by sex, age, seriousness of offense, or any other criteria. The building usually had a single fireplace for heat, and if inmates' families or some other source of charity did not provide wood, those confined were without heat. The inmates could buy food from the jailer, if they had money, or if they could get friends or charity to donate it. Those who were rich could have meals prepared and brought to the jail. There are also instances in which those with economic resources could stay at an inn in lieu of the jail. Those with money had privileges even in the colonial days, and it was not uncommon for the indigent inmate to die in jail because of his lack of resources.

In England there had been a fee system in which prisoners were charged for being locked up. This fee system continued to be used after independence in the United States and persisted in some areas well into the twentieth century. Fees went to the jailer and, if handled astutely, could result in tidy profits to him.

Along with jails, workhouses and houses of correction were also built. In some instances they performed the functions that had been initially assigned to them in England. However, at different times and locations, the functions and roles of these facilities were altered, merged, and confused.

Even in England at this time the functions of the workhouse and house of correction were blurring, and this lack of distinction was transplanted to the colonies. Among the early confinement facilities built in America, the workhouse was sometimes used as and called a house of correction, and the house of correction was often used as and called a workhouse. This practice persisted into the twentieth century. Often these facilities were located next to or even within the jail and were in many cases admininstered by the jailer. The

geographical closeness of the institution, as well as the dual administration, threw additional confusion into the minds of the public.

When in America a pure workhouse was built, that is, as it was
originally developed in England, it was used for those who were
unemployed but willing to work. Stocks of materials were supplied
these individuals, and the inmates were paid for the finished
products. This practice also continued in some areas into the twentieth century.

Houses of correction were constructed in various colonial areas
also, but their inmates were often in a different category from those
confined in them in England, even though the concept was of
English origin. In 1658 the colony of New Plymouth provided for
the construction of a workhouse or house of correction for Quakers,
idle persons, vagrants, rebellious children, and difficult servants. As
Robinson says, "No better evidence of the transplanting of the
house of correction and the workhouse from England to America is
needed than the Act of May 31, 1699, of the Massachusetts Bay
Colony, entitled, 'An Act for suppression and punishing of Rogues,
Vagabonds, common Beggars, and other lewd, idle and disorderly
Persons. And also for setting the Poor to Work.' "[10] Much of the
language of this decree closely resembled the English laws of the
same period.

In 1682 William Penn's "Great Law" was adopted. To this law
there was an addition that in 1683 stipulated that all prisons should
be workhouses for "felons, thieves, vagrants and loose, abusive and
idle persons." Thus, in Penn's colony, the jail (or workhouse) was
designed to incarcerate convicted criminals, debtors, and vagrants,
and so assumed the role of holding those convicted of crimes. The
jail had now become principally a place for the detention of convicted offenders (there may be some dispute whether these were jails
or workhouses and it may, therefore, continue to be a problem of
semantics). Penn's more humanitarian treatment of criminals did
not last long. At his death in 1718 the Great Law was abolished,
and the harsher English criminal law was reintroduced. Pennsylvania facilities soon sank to a low level; it was for a future
generation to return to Penn's reform movement.

In the beginning American jails usually were places to detain
people awaiting trial, although there were some initial alterations of

this policy in different colonies. Later, when corporal punishment was under attack, the jail in some areas was used to imprison such convicted petty offenders as drunks and vagrants. At the beginning of the eighteenth century jails also began to hold convicted political and religious offenders as well as debtors. As in Pennsylvania, such people could have been confined in workhouse-jail combinations or in regular jails. The point is not clear. But with the events of the seventeenth century in Pennsylvania and these new developments, the jail was beginning to alter its function.

5

Walnut Street Jail and the Period of Change

A turning point occurred in confinement facilities and attitudes around the time of the American Revolution. Up to that period there were essentially three institutions that were part of the American criminal justice system. First, there were jails, with their early English origin. Second to be invented was the house of correction, often confused with and often serving the same function as the third institution, the workhouse. To this group of confinement facilities would be added a fourth, that of the prison.[1]

The foundations for development of the prison in America had been laid during the late seventeenth century and the eighteenth century. The prison was, in fact, the inevitable outcome of societal forces. One of the most important factors in the development of prisons was the colonists' attitude toward the harsh English legal system. Many of those who had settled in the New World had spent time in English jails, some for various ideological and social beliefs. Once they settled in the New World they tended to reject the harsh treatment given to offenders in England.[2]

This is not to say that colonial jails were excellent examples of man's humanity to man; however, it does appear that prisoners were treated better as a whole than elsewhere, and that legal sanctions were not as harsh as they could have been. During the colonial period there were many capital offenses for which one could be put to death. Judges and juries, however, became reluctant to hand out the death penalty, and consequently, many who were guilty were found innocent and released.

In addition to this mood found in the colonies, there was also a movement in Europe toward general humanitarian reform, which undoubtedly had some effect upon the early colonists, but more important was the change in much of Europe itself. Many of the early evils were assailed in the writings of French philosophers such as Montesquieu, Voltaire, Diderot, Turgot, and Condorcet. In England, social conditions were attacked by David Hume, Adam Smith, Thomas Paine, and Jeremy Bentham. These men attempted to introduce rationalism into both the political and social philosophy of the time. They proclaimed that a better social order could be achieved through the use of reason. "They upheld man as the supreme achievement of God's creative ingenuity and emphasized his importance more than any previous thinkers, save some of the Greeks and Romans and a few of the more radical humanists of the Renaissance."[3]

There were also specific reforms aimed at criminal jurisprudence and penal administration. In addition to John Howard and Jeremy Bentham, there were men like Sir Samuel Romilly, Sir William Blackstone, Pope Clement XI, and the most famous, Cesare Beccaria. All played vital parts in activating European reform movements in various social areas.

Besides rejecting in theory harsh treatment, the colonists had amongst them many social activists. From the onset, the Quakers had pushed for confinement reform. Probably their greatest achievement up to the War of Independence was the program under William Penn. These reforms, although short lived, were dramatic. The seeds for change in America were planted and awaited the time for growth.

Immediately after the Revolution the forces for change sprouted under the leadership of such men as Benjamin Rush, Benjamin Franklin, William Bradford, Caleb Lownes, Bishop William White, Roberts Vaux, and Richard Vaux. These men were also influenced by the many foreign travelers who came to the United States during the Revolutionary War. Among the ranks of visitors were a number of Frenchmen with humanitarian ideals.[4]

Probably one of the most influential organizations for criminal confinement reform developed in the Philadelphia Society for Alleviating the Miseries of Public Prisons. This organization contained many Quakers, but was initially led by Bishop White, first president of the Protestant Episcopal Church. The society began in 1787 as the Philadelphia Society for Assisting Distressed Persons and is currently called the Pennsylvania Prison Society.[5]

Reform after the Revolution was aimed not only at the confinement institutions but also at the criminal code. The Quakers contended that the sole end of punishment was the prevention of crime. They believed that punishment as it was being inflicted was degrading, cruel, and tyrannical. The punishment should fit the crime, and the prison should be a penitentiary where persons could reflect upon their crimes and emerge as better men and women, rather than more vicious and perverted.[6]

In reforming the criminal code, alternative sanctions had to be developed in lieu of capital punishment, whipping, branding, and other forms of brutality. Prison was substituted for many of these earlier forms of punishment. It was seen as a system that would take the place of jails and workhouses. Neither of the latter was secure or good for long-term employment. "Thus, the desire for greater security and the hope of using prison labor were two important immediate motives for the creation of state prisons."[7]

One of the earliest known prisons to handle felons was established in 1773 in Simsbury, Connecticut. An abandoned copper mine was used, and inmates were kept in the long mine shafts. Administration buildings were located near the entrances. This represents one of several American attempts to both house and work the convicted felon.[8] Known as the Newgate Prison, it was not much better than the sulphur pits of early Rome and was replaced by the prison at Wethersfield in 1827. Incidentally, in 1774 Newgate Prison was the scene of the first prison riot in America. It never became an important confinement facility in the United States.

Pennsylvania, under the Quaker influence, established the first prison in America of any significance. Due to legislative acts in Pennsylvania from 1789 to 1794, the Walnut Street Jail was converted from a jail to a prison. The Act of 1790 produced the beginning of the modern prison concept in the United States. This act ". . . established the principle of solitary confinement upon which the Pennsylvania system and later the Auburn system of prison discipline were based, and it provided for remodeling the Walnut Street Jail in accord with this principle. Convicts in solitary confinement were not allowed out of their cells either for work or recreation, although the other convicts worked together in shops during the day."[9]

Many of the ideas incorporated into the new prison came from Europe, where solitary confinement (cellular construction) and work programs were already practiced. For ten years the Walnut Street Jail system functioned well, and it soon became a model for other prisons. By the end of 1817, the states of New York, Kentucky, New Jersey, Virginia, Massachusetts, Maryland, Vermont, New Hampshire, Ohio, and Georgia had used the Walnut Street Jail as a model on which to build their own prisons. However, the Walnut Street Jail itself disappeared in the first part of the nineteenth century, due to overcrowding, politics, incompetent personnel, prisoner idleness, and lack of financial support.[10]

Knowledge of American jail confinement practices during this period of prison development is very scant. The legal status of criminals did not change everywhere at one time. The movement in the United States was toward reform, but the reform apparently did not touch the jails. In many instances, they remained the same deplorable places they had always been. The changes were directed at posttrial conditions in criminal justice procedures rather than pretrial confinement and, furthermore, were directed toward the posttrial confinement problems of the more serious offenders rather than toward the petty offenders.

It is nonetheless important to trace briefly the development of the early prisons, since many of the practices as well as the architecture can be found in later jails. Although the jail is a unique institution with its own set of problems and circumstances, much of the influence of confinement philosophies and architecture has been from the prisons to the jails.

In 1817 the Philadelphia Society for Alleviating the Miseries of Public Prisons began to work for the reorganization of prisons of Pennsylvania. Legislation enacted in 1818 and 1821 provided for solitary confinement in prisons without employment. A new prison was authorized, to be located at Pittsburgh and designed by William Strickland, who had been greatly influenced by Bentham's Panoptican.[11] The new prison, known as the Western Penitentiary, opened in 1826 and became the first important prison in the United States to have complete individual housing in separate cells.

The Pittsburgh prison was soon followed by another (1829) on the other side of the state, the Eastern Penitentiary, located at Cherry Hill in Philadelphia. This penitentiary was designed by John Haviland and "combined the radiating cell blocks of the Ghent Workhouse and the outside cells of the Papal house of correction of Saint Michael in Rome."[12] The Philadelphia prison soon became the model to be followed by others.

Inmates of the Eastern Penitentiary spent most of their prison time in their cells, where they read the Bible and religious tracts and received moral instruction. The cells in this penitentiary were eleven feet, nine inches long, seven feet six inches wide, and sixteen feet high; and each had two doors, one leading to the corridor and the other to an exercise yard. Prisoners were allowed out of their cells for one hour each day to exercise in a solitary, high-walled exercise yard where they could have no contacts with other inmates.

Shortly after the Eastern Penitentiary was opened, the legislature changed the law and provided for solitary labor in the cells in the two prisons. Inmates were required to work at such activities as carpentry, weaving, tailoring, and shoemaking.

These new approaches in the Western and Eastern penitentiaries became known as the Pennsylvania system or the "separate system." However, this separate system of prayer, meditation, and work to accomplish reformation was soon challenged by Louis Dwight and his Boston Prison Discipline Society.[13] They suggested that the inmates be allowed to work together in silence rather than in isolation. They felt that by allowing inmates to work together they could avoid the horrors of silence. By 1823 the prison at Auburn, New York, was built, and the new proposal was inaugurated. Since enforcing silence when men were together was a problem, the warden set up a rigid system of discipline and repression. "Outside of their cells inmates were forbidden not only to speak to each other, but to look at each other face to face: visual communication might lead to gesturing, gesturing to whispering. To ensure that the looks of prisoners would not meet, they were required to walk with downcast eyes, to remain in constant activity when outside of their cells, and, when traveling from location to location in groups, to march in a peculiarly shortened, heavy gait known as the lock step. Violation of any of these or a large number of other regulations could bring punishment by flogging.[14]

At Auburn the cells were placed back to back in tiers within a large building with a door opening upon galleries eight to ten feet from the outer walls. This was the origin of the interior cellblock that is characteristic of some of the jails and most of the prisons in the United States.

Although the Auburn and Pennsylvania systems were similar, a controversy developed over them from 1825 to 1860 which became quite intense. On the Auburn side was the Prison Discipline Society of Boston and on the side of the Pennsylvania system was the Philadelphia Society for Alleviating the Miseries of Public Prisons. Both sides distorted statistics and were extremely subjective about their evaluations.

The supporters of the Pennsylvania system claimed: "(1) that it facilitated the control of prisoners, (2) that it permitted greater consideration of their individual needs, (3) that it prevented contamination through contact with other convicts, (4) that it provided opportunity for meditation and repentance, and (5) that it secured relative anonymity upon discharge.[15]

In reply to these charges, the advocates of the Auburn system contended: "(1) that it was cheaper to introduce, (2) that it provided greater opportunity for vocational training, and (3) that it produced more revenue for the state."[16]

Both sides, of course, had their weaknesses and strengths, but eventually, except in the state of Pennsylvania, the Auburn system predominated in the United States. Most of the new prisons followed programs, rules, and punishments like Auburn's and had similar architecture.

From the time of the conversion of the Walnut Street Jail to a prison, various prisons began to be constructed in different states. The new emphasis on reforms was directed at the prisons and the serious offenders. Interest in the different classes of misdemeanants waned, and conditions in jails lost the reformers' interest. The jails, workhouses, and houses of correction continued to exist, but there were few people concerned with their conditions or that of their inmates. This shift in concern away from the jails had a profound and lasting effect upon these institutions—an effect that is evident today.

6

Nineteenth-Century American Jails

In the nineteenth century notable changes took place in the function of jails. "The jails now had to house not only those detained awaiting trial but also those who had been convicted."[1] In most circumstances, felons or more serious offenders had been sentenced to the newly developed state prisons. But some states developed few, if any, prisons. In many of the Southern states individuals convicted of serious offenses were either executed or confined to county jails for long periods of time.

The stocks, pillory, whipping posts, and dunking stools were beginning to leave the American scene. They did not disappear from every part of the country all at once, but there were efforts aimed at decreasing their use. Prior to the Civil War, for example, North Carolina had fifteen offenses punishable by placement in the pillory or by whipping or both. But corporal punishment on an official basis was declining.

Changes in conditions and functions in the jail did not take place in all jails at the same time.[2] Jails were locally operated and consequently affected by local matters. The speed with which a jail changed or initiated a new practice seemed to be subject not only to legislation but also to local, state, and regional considerations. Some jails changed overnight, but others took many decades to change even in the smallest way. Change was not (and is not) a phenomenon that takes place equally everywhere.

Jails in many places at the turn of the century housed those awaiting trial, those serving sentences, and in some locations those held as material witnesses. Scattered among this population were children, debtors, slaves, and both the mentally and physically ill. Most were housed in facilities, which if not old and dilapidated, were constructed with little concern for their inhabitants. Jails were cold, dark, dirty, crowded, and lacked in most cases even rudimentary sanitary conditions or facilities. They were poor places to visit and even worse in which to be incarcerated.

Debtors who had played such a prominent role in the jail population began to disappear from it. Debt in colonial America had been an offense for which one could be imprisoned. The laws pertaining to it were spelled out quite clearly as this 1830 summary of the Massachusetts statutes indicate:

> The property exempt from attachment is the wearing apparel, beds, bedsteads, bedding and household utensils, of any debtor necessary for himself, wife and children; the tools of any debtor, necessary for his trade or occupation; the Bibles and school books which may be in actual use in his or her family, together with one cow and one swine; provided, that the beds and bedding, exempted as aforesaid, shall not exceed one bed, bedstead, and necessary bedding for two persons; and household furniture, the value of fifty dollars.
>
> By a subsequent law, the following articles are added to the foregoing, viz: six sheep, and two tons of hay for the use of said sheep, and for the use of a cow: said sheep, however, are not to exceed in value the sum of thirty dollars.
>
> By a still later law, all cast-iron or sheet-iron stoves, used exclusively for the purpose of warming buildings, are exempted; provided, that not more than one such stove to each building, occupied by the same person or family, shall be so exempted.
>
> Body of the debtor liable to arrest and commitment to jail, on mesne process and execution, for any sum where the debt or damage shall exceed the sum of five dollars.
>
> Where the debt or damage does not exceed five dollars, the body cannot be arrested; property only can be taken.
>
> When the body of the debtor shall be committed to close confinement in any Jail, he shall be furnished with an apartment separate from that occupied by *criminals*.
>
> Jail yards are not to extend more than fifty rods from the Jail.

Any person imprisoned for debt, either upon mesne process or execution, shall be allowed the liberties of the Jail yard, on giving bond, with sufficient surety or sureties, to the creditor or creditors, in double the sum for which he is imprisoned, conditioned that he will not depart from the Prison limits.

Bail may at any time surrender the principal, and be discharged from any further liability.

Whenever any person, committed to Jail on execution for debt, shall wish to avail himself of the benefit of the act for the relief of poor debtors, by taking the poor debtor's oath, and thereupon being discharged from his imprisonment, he must make application to some justice of the peace, who shall thereupon issue a notice to the creditor or creditors, his or their attorney, &c., *thirty days* previous to the time appointed for his being admitted to said oath.

If, after examination had before the proper authorities, the debtor shall be admitted to and shall take said oath, he shall thereupon be discharged from his imprisonment.

Such discharge does not at all affect the claim of the creditor on any property the debtor may subsequently possess. The body of the debtor, however, can never be afterwards arrested for the same debt or demand.

If any town shall become liable for the support of any poor prisoner in Jail, said town may recover any expense, so incurred, of the creditor who imprisoned him.

Neither jailer or other person is permitted to give or furnish any spirituous liquor to persons committed to Jail, either for debt or for crime.

No person committed to prison *on execution* for debt, if not discharged from his imprisonment within ninety days from his commitment, shall be allowed to have the liberties of the yard for a greater length of time than ninety days; but shall be put in close confinement, and be so continued until discharged from prison by the creditor, or in due course of law.[3]

Later it became more difficult to jail an individual for this offense alone, and by the mid-nineteenth century imprisonment for debt was generally abolished.

During the earlier part of the century there was also some increased concern for the plight of children who were confined in jails. Up to this time they were thrown into jail for offenses including the most trivial, and were confined unsegregated with men and women of varying criminal records. If they had not learned about crime before their confinement, they would most certainly learn about it while there.

The first facility solely dedicated to housing juveniles who were in conflict with the law was the House of Refuge established in 1825 in New York City. This building, a barracks leased from the government, stood where Madison Square Garden is presently located. The object was to protect children from vice, poverty, and neglect, and to guide them to a better life.

The House of Refuge was followed by the House of Reformation in Boston in 1826 and the Philadelphia House of Refuge in 1828. Such houses signaled the beginning movements aimed at removing children from jails.[4] These three facilities were founded and administered with private funds and it wasn't until 1847, with the opening of the Westborough, Massachusetts, reform school for boys, that a state reformatory was established, the first public institution of its kind in America.[5] Despite the fact that these early institutions were headed by educators and presumably men of vision, they were little better than the jails they attempted to replace. They retained much of the atmosphere found in the other facilities of the time.

Children continued to be housed in jails throughout the nineteenth century, a practice that persists even now. However, as the nineteenth century progressed, a trend developed in which children were separated from the male inmates. In some of these facilities the juveniles were placed with women inmates, while in other places they were segregated and placed adjacent to the women's wards.

Even in the twentieth century there is no clear-cut pattern pertaining to children in jails, but there seems to be a trend to remove them completely from such facilities. As the years passed fewer and fewer juveniles were confined in jail. Increasingly, they were kept in a completely separate section of the jail because the county or city lacked separate juvenile facilities. They were temporarily transferred to jails if they had severe behavior problems and were then likely to stay there until their hearings or the disposition of their case. It is rare in the twentieth century to find juveniles serving sentences in jails.

In Boston the Children's Aid Society visited the jails where large numbers of children were confined and distributed religious tracts and pious advice. In 1864 the society persuaded a friend, Rufus R. Cook to visit the jails and screen out those cases that looked as if they could profit from other placement. Those whom he felt would benefit from other arrangements were removed while those who couldn't were presumably left in jail. The released children were sent to private institutions and to the new public ones.[6]

During the Civil War the adult population in the jails generally declined but juvenile jail population in the North increased. The reason for this is not clear, but the increase did occur. The extent is difficult to establish, since few jails kept complete statistics.

In the South, even after the Civil War, in contrast to the North, reform schools were not established. Because of the poor conditions found in jails the authorities were often reluctant to confine children there, and consequently they were often pardoned. Nevertheless, many children did serve time in jail not only in the South but in the rest of the country as well.

In 1865, Franklin B. Sanborn, secretary of the Massachusetts Board of State Charities, noted an increase in the number of juveniles confined in the jails of his state and commented that, "Among them . . . mere infants . . . such as the one I found in Plymouth House of Correction, sentenced to thirty days imprisonment—and he only six years old."[7] Although the number of juvenile facilities increased toward the end of the nineteenth century, children continued to serve their sentences in jails in most areas of the nation.

Many jail and prison reforms of the first half of the nineteenth century were probably related to the greater openness of Jacksonian democracy and the efforts of some scattered reform groups. The best known of these groups was the Prison Discipline Society of Boston. This society was concerned with "every class subjected to confinement in prison, the criminal, debtor and the insane." Its reports were edited and distributed by its ambitious leader, the Reverend Louis Dwight. These reports, issued from 1829 to 1855, present us with some of the only available material on jails of that period.[8] Although many of them were somewhat subjective in order to serve the aims of the society and did favor the Auburn approach to incarceration, they provide at least a partial view of the jails of the period.

There was not a typical jail in the United States during the nineteenth century and for that matter there still isn't a typical jail even now. They were and are quite diverse in size, condition, population, structure, and management.

The size of the nineteenth century jails varied greatly. There were those built for only one or two inmates and those that could house hundreds. In the 1820s, those jails located in Boston, New York, Philadelphia, Baltimore, Washington D.C., Richmond, Charleston, and New Orleans generally held from 700 to 1,000 persons each.[9]

An 1834 report by the Prison Discipline Society reveals the variety and size of some of the Massachusetts jails and houses of correction. The report, which was concerned with disregard of the principle of solitary confinement at night, reviewed the size of these facilities and their inmate populations.

> *Lenox Jail, Sept. 24, 1833*—Room No. 1; six men in this room; three white and three colored; among them, one poor lunatic, furiously mad. Room No. 2, unoccupied. Two cells, in the same story, used for correcting misdemeanor in the Prison, and for no other purpose. Room No. 5; five persons in this room, all white men. Room No. 6; one colored female, the only one in the Prison. Room No. 7, unoccupied. Four rooms in the third story, all used for debtors; at this time unoccupied. Eleven rooms, and twelve prisoners, and all the prisoners in three rooms.
>
> *Springfield Jail, Sept. 26, 1833*—Fifteen apartments in the Jail, and only four prisoners; two for debt, who occupy the same room; one man for crime, who is confined alone; and one colored woman, a poor lunatic, at this time furiously mad, also confined alone.
>
> *Northampton Jail, Sept. 27, 1833*—Room No. 1, and the dungeon, unoccupied. Room No. 2, unoccupied. Roon No. 3, unoccupied. Room No. 4, occupied by a man aged forty-two, committed for selling ardent spirits, and a boy, aged thirteen, committed for stealing. The boy *was* alone, in the north room, about three weeks, but does not like that. Room No. 5, unoccupied. Room No. 6, unoccupied. Room No. 7, occupied by one debtor. Seven rooms, and three prisoners; a man and a boy, unfit associates, placed together, when there are rooms enough unoccupied.
>
> *Greenfield Jail, Sept. 28, 1833*—This Jail was built on the

principle of solitary confinement; and the principle appears to be adhered to rigidly, except in regard to debtors.

Worcester Jail, Oct. 1, 1833—Room No. 1, and the dungeon, Nos. 2, 3, 4, and 5, unoccupied. Room No. 6, occupied by two prisoners; one for stealing a horse, and one for stealing money; both untried. Room No. 7, occupied by one prisoner. Room No. 8, occupied by one prisoner.

Worcester House of Correction—This house has been altered so as to adapt it to the principle of solitary confinement, at night; and the principle appears to be rigidly adhered to.

Boston Jail, Oct. 15, 1833—South building, lower story, room No. 1; three prisoners; one, untried, for assault, expects his trial at the Municipal Court; one, as a common drunkard, has had his trial, and is now confined on fine and costs; and one, a Spaniard, for fighting, has had his trial, and is now confined on fine and costs. Rooms Nos. 2, 3, 4, and 5, unoccupied. Room No. 6; two prisoners, both for attempting to kill; one has not had his trial and the other is confined on fine and costs. Rooms Nos. 7, 8, and 9, unoccupied.—Second story, Room No.1, occupied by two prisoners: one for fighting, and one as a common drunkard. Room No. 2, occupied by two prisoners; one young man, for stealing an umbrella, and sentenced for twenty days, and an old man, for drunkenness, on fine and costs. Rooms Nos. 3, 4, 5, 7, 8, and 9, unoccupied. Room No. 6, used as a storeroom.—Third story, used for debtors. Room No. 1, one debtor. Room No. 2, two debtors. Room No. 3, two debtors. Room No. 4, three debtors. Room No. 5, three colored men for debt. Room No. 6, three debtors. Room No. 7, three debtors. Room No. 8, one debtor. Room No. 9, four debtors.—In the two lower stories, used for criminals, eighteen rooms, nine prisoners occupying only four rooms, and fourteen rooms unoccupied.

House of Correction, at South Boston, Oct. 17, 1833—This establishment was refitted, on the principle of solitary confinement at night, and the principle is adhered to.

Dedham Jail, Oct. 23, 1833—Rooms Nos. 1, 2, 3, 4, 5, 6, and 7, unoccupied. Room No. 8, occupied by one criminal; and room No. 9, by one debtor.

House of Correction, in Dedham—This establishment was built on the principle of solitary confinement at night, and the principle is adhered to.

Taunton Jail, Oct. 24, 1833—Rooms Nos. 1, 2, 3, 4, 6, 7, 8, 9, 10, 11, and 12, unoccupied. Room No. 5, occupied by one young female, for larceny, who has been in Prison before; and Room No. 13, directly over it, into which there is a hole dug through the ceiling and floor, occupied by two prisoners; one an old man, aged about sixty years, for fighting, who has been in this Prison before, and the other a young man, for taking a coat. Thirteen rooms, and only three prisoners; two of these in one room, and all three in rooms so connected that they might almost as well be in the same room.

New Bedford Jail and House of Correction, Oct. 29, 1833—This establishment was built on the principle of solitary confinement at night; but, in its management at this time, all good principles of Prison discipline appear to have been rejected.

Barnstable Jail, Oct. 27, 1833—Room No. 1; three prisoners, all concerned in the riot at Provincetown, in which Thomas Rogers was murdered; all young men, from nineteen to twenty-one years of age. Room No. 2, unoccupied. Room No. 3, occupied by four young men, from eighteen to twenty years of age; all concerned in the riot at Provincetown, in which Rogers was killed.—Room No. 2, occupied by one poor paralytic; and Room No. 3, occupied by two prisoners, one a youth of seventeen, and the other a man of twenty-nine, both committed for stealing.—Six rooms in this Prison, and ten prisoners, and only four rooms occupied.

Nantucket Jail, Oct. 26, 1833—Room No. 1, occupied by two prisoners, one a Frenchman, thirty-six years of age; has had his trial, and is performing his sentence, for stealing; the other a youth of fourteen, who has, also, has his trial, and is performing his sentence, for stealing. Room No. 2, unoccupied. —Room No. 1, second story, occupied by a youth of eighteen. Room No. 2, same story, occupied by a debtor. Four rooms in this prison, and four prisoners, occupying three rooms.

Edgartown Jail, Oct. 26, 1833—Four rooms, all unoccupied.

Plymouth Jail, Oct. 31, 1833—Rooms Nos. 1, 2, 3, and 4, unoccupied. Room No. 5, occupied by one young man, accused of murder; his situation is favorable for repentance.—Rooms Nos. 1, 3, and 4, second story, unoccupied. Room No. 2, occupied by two debtors.—Eight rooms, and three prisoners, occupying two rooms.

Cambridge Jail, at Lechmere Point, Oct. 18, 1833—Room No. 1, occupied, at night, by four prisoners; two in a bed. Room No. 2, occupied, at night, by four prisoners; two in a bed. Rooms Nos. 3 and 4, never occupied, on account of their construction.—Room No. 1, second story, occupied by two prisoners; one an Irishman, who has been tried and found guilty of stealing, and one young American, who is accused of stealing; but has not had his trial. Here the tried and untried are together. Room No. 2, same story, occupied by two prisoners; one accused of the murder of his wife, and the other of being concerned largely in counterfeiting; neither of them have been tried. Room No. 3, occupied by three prisoners, at night. Room No. 4, occupied by three prisoners.—Room No. 1, third story, occupied by one female. Room No. 2, occupied by two females; one for adultery, and one for intemperance. Room No. 3, occupied by three debtors. Room No. 4, occupied by three debtors.—Twelve rooms, ten only fit for use, and twenty-eight prisoners; necessarily, therefore, crowded together at night.

Concord Jail, Nov. 13, 1833—Room No. 1, occupied by four prisoners, in two beds. Room No. 2, occupied by three prisoners; one of them a wretch, who has been in this Jail five times, and as often, the jailer says, in the Jail at Cambridge, for abusing his family. One of the other prisoners complains bitterly of being in the same room with him. Room No. 3, and the dungeon connected with it, unoccupied. Room No. 4, occupied by four prisoners; one negro giant, aged twenty-eight years, for adultery, on sentence for one year; one young man, aged eighteen, on fine and costs, has been clerk in a store at Lowell; one young man, aged twenty-one, on fine and costs; and one man, aged twenty-seven, who has been for a long time familiarly acquainted with the arts and practices of counterfeiters, and has been largely concerned in the business. It is difficult to conceive of a more dangerous association than this.—Room No. 1, second story, occupied by two debtors; one aged twenty-one, and the other nineteen: the former says he was not twenty-one when he signed the note, as surety for a friend, on which he is now in Prison. Room No. 2, same story, occupied by two debtors. Room No. 3, occupied by two prisoners; one a youth of seventeen, from Boston, on fine and costs; and one an Irishman, aged twenty-four, on fine and costs, for fighting. Room No. 4, occupied by one prisoner.—Eight rooms, in the third story, all unoccupied, because the windows are not grated; and, in other respects, they would not be sufficiently secure, except for debtors.—Eight rooms, not including the eight in the upper story, which are unfit for use, and eighteen prisoners; necessarily, therefore, having two or more in a room.[10]

The populations of the jails differed depending upon the geographical location being considered, with the House of Correction at South Boston probably being typical of that area. Tables 6.1 and 6.2 show statistics for that institution in 1837.

Table 6.1 **Number of Prisoners Confined May 1, 1837**
South Boston House of Correction

Sex	Race		Total
	White	Black	
Males	145	13	158
Females	59	10	69
Total	204	23	227

Table 6.2 **Number of Recidivists for the Year Ending**
May 1, 1837, South Boston House of Correction

Number of Recommitments	Number of Persons	
	Male	Female
1	26	26
2	19	16
3	9	8
4	7	8
5	6	5
6	6	6
7	4	3
8	2	1
9	1	2
10 or more	4	12
Total	84	87

Total number of persons recommitted: 171
SOURCE: *Prison Discipline Society Report 12, 1837.*

During the year preceding May 1, 1837, a total of 579 people had been committed. Of these, 284 were "foreigners" and 295 were Americans. Seven people who died in the House of Correction were described as "persons aged and infirm, with worn-down constitutions."[11]

There were many causes for commitment to Boston's House of Correction. For example, the 158 males incarcerated on May 1, 1837, were committed for the following offenses:

Common and notorious thieves	2
Felonious assault	1
Assault	1
Assault on a child 10 years old and attempt to rape	1
Adultery	1
Larceny	49
Larceny in a dwelling place	6
Common drunkards	64
Common drunkards & vagabonds	5
Vagabonds	11
Lascivious & common drunkard	1
Resisting constable	3
Forgery	1
Escape from House of Correction	2
Lunatic	10
Total	158

For females the offenses were somewhat different:

Passing Counterfeit money	1
Larceny in a dwelling house	1
Larceny	15
Wanton and lascivious	10
Common drunkards & vagabonds	3
Night-walkers	3
Common drunkards & night-walkers	5
Keeping a brothel	2
Vagabond	1
Common drunkards	23
Escaping from House of Correction	1
Lunatics	4
Total	69

Most prisoners in the South Boston House of Correction were required to work. Male prisoners on May 1, 1837, were employed in the following manner:

Cutting stone	40
Blacksmiths	6
Workmen in brass and nail foundry	16
Hat shop	8
Taylors	2
Shoemakers	4
Bakers	2
Stone-cutters, masons, blacksmiths, and other employed on the West Wing Prison	20
Carpenters and laborers at the House of Reformation	20
Aged and sick employed in garden, picking wood, attending Prison yard, lunatics and hospital	23
Lunatics and idiots	12
Sick in hospital	5

The women in this institution were "employed in making jackets, pantaloons, and skirts, and contract Prison garments." They also cooked for the prisoners and served as domestics in the jailer's house. In addition, some of them worked binding hats and shoes.

At about the same time this survey was made, Hartford, Connecticut, built a new county jail considered so good that the Prison Discipline Society termed it "the best model County Prison in the country." Alfred Smith, who was instrumental in having this county prison constructed, wrote the following letter to the society:

Hartford, 2d March, 1837.

Dear sir,

From June, 1827, to March, 1835, 386 prisoners were confined in the County Jail here, the major part being persons detained for trial, the residue under sentence for minor offences. The average was 50 persons a year, confined for crime, or to be tried for crime. The time of confinement varied from a few days to two or three and, rarely, six months. The average was four and a half weeks to each of the 386 prisoners. Part of them were discharged on the expiration of their sentence, part were not brought to trial, or were acquitted, two were executed, and the rest sent to the State Prison at Wethersfield.

The number of debtors brought to Jail, during the same period of seven years and nine months, was 1121, but few of whom were confined within the Prison, most of them being bailed out, and living and lodging, as our laws permit, anywhere in the city, at their pleasure.

At times, the number in Prison is very small. Often, it is from 6 to 10 or 12, rarely 15 or 20; and once only, (in 1834), 30 prisoners were confined in this Jail at the same time.

Amongst the prisoners are old and young, male and female, white and colored, petty trespassers and pilferers, and adroit and daring villains, incendiaries, housebreakers, counterfeiters, murders, &c. Some were insane, others weak almost to idiocy. This state has no Hospital for the confinement of persons acquitted on the ground of insanity, and such persons can only be sent to the County Jails.

The old Jail had a tavern under the same roof. The building formed a corner, by two public streets, and was without any enclosure; contained seven Prison rooms, large and small, which were approached by dark and crooked passages, and which enabled Teller and Caesar (confined for murder) to lock in the keeper and his guard, to get from the Prison into the house; and, but for a timely rally of the neighborhood, they would have escaped.

The old Prison was warmed by stoves in the rooms, and was formerly burnt. An insane female prisoner, excited by some mockery of persons outside, kindled the fire and perished in the flames.

By means of strings let down from the Prison windows, files, saws, and other things, could be, and often were, conveyed to prisoners.

Your acquaintance with Prisons will enable you to perceive, at a glance, the means by which the defects of the old Prison are avoided or remedied. The County Jail has no guard or night-watch, like a State Prison. The grated door and window (*i* and *m*) are intended to enable the keeper or his assistant to inspect the Prison, and hear any noise therein, by night and day, and whether in his office or bedroom, without being obliged to enter the Prison. The cells are large enough to work in, and light enough. The are [sic] would be a safe place to employ some of the prisoners, who might be overlooked from the office. In a County Jail, a keeper, with some mechanical trade, could employ his time profitably, and might use his office to work in.

The new Prison lot contains about two acres, bounded south and west by Little River, north by a highway, east by private property. The house fronts towards the north, is set back 35 feet from the road, and there is room for ample Prison yards, should such be required.

Double doors, from paving to ceiling, are to be put across the north area, between *m* and *n*, and single doors across the south area, to close and serve as partitions in winter, and throw entirely open in summer. Their use is to save fuel and warming, when only one side of the Prison is occupied, as there are *generally* fewer than 16 prisoners confined at once.

The Prison rooms in the house part (*t,u,v*) are intended for debtors, or females, or sick, or insane, as occasion may require.

You inquire if any improvements have occurred to me. No material ones in the plan, for this county and location. I think it would be more convenient to have the Prison windows rise and fall by weights, instead of opening in halves from top to bottom, although the latter opens twice as much of the area to the open air—Some might prefer to place the first floor of the cells on a level with the floor of the keeper's office,—thus giving all the stairs to the second story of cells. Something may depend on the site. In our case, it diminished the expense, to keep the floors down; and perhaps the keeper has both stories of cells more perfectly under his observation, as they are here arranged, than if the first floor of the cells were brought up to the level of the keeper's office floor.

The cells are of brick, with stone caps and sills. A rabbit is formed for the door by throwing eight inches, of the twenty of brick-work, forward two inches. The cell doors shut twelve inches within the face of the wall, and open outward. I should prefer stone jambs, and think that the expense need not be much increased. I enclose a form of stone jambs, which can be varied so as to make the front of the cells nearly as strong as solid stone-work; and a grated door of equal dimensions would admit eight or ten percent more light, if fitted to a rabbit cut in stone jambs, than where they project, like ours, two inches.

The new Jail and County House were erected by contract, at an agreed price of rather less than 10,300 dollars, exclusive of Prison irons. The weight and cost of these is not yet entirely ascertained. They will probably amount, including doors, grates, sliding-bars, levers, locks, bedsteads, &c., to about 4,000 dollars more; besides which, there are wells, vaults, furniture, &c.

I enclose the drawing and description which you requested, and expect soon to convey them by a private hand. You can use the whole or part, and if any thing material is omitted, I will endeavor to supply it, when pointed out.

With great respect and regard,
Your obedient servant,
ALFRED SMITH.[12]

Congregate confinement — England. Courtesy U.S. Bureau of Prisons.

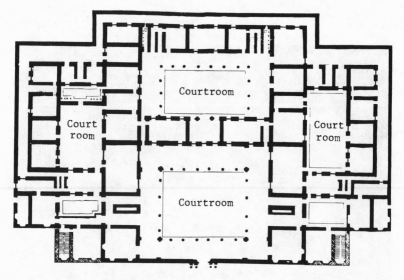

Plan of a new jail in Milan (c. 1624) as presented in Serafino Biffi's *Sulle Antiche Carceri de Milano.*

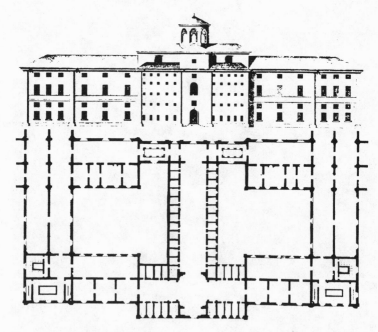

Plan of the Milan House of Corrections (c. 1756) as presented in John Howard's *State of the Prisons.*

John Howard — English prison reformer.
Courtesy U.S. Bureau of Prisons.

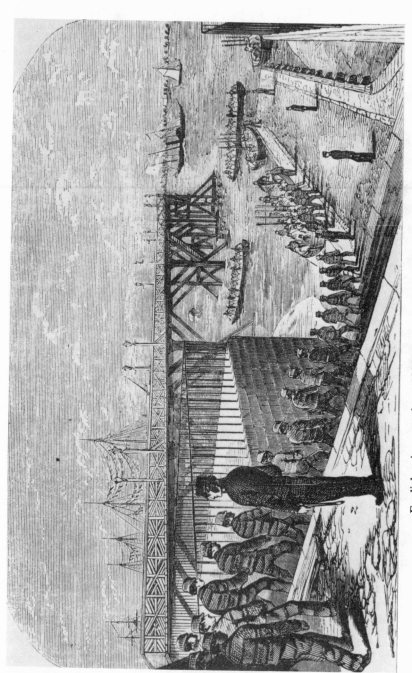

English prisoners about 1825. Courtesy U.S. Bureau of Prisons.

An English Hulk. Courtesy U.S. Bureau of Prisons.

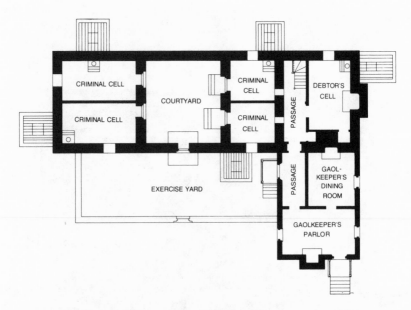

Public gaol, Williamsburg, Virginia, as it appeared c. 1722.

Stock and whipping post, Williamsburg gaol.

Old Simsbury Mines Prison — first prison in the U.S. Courtesy U.S. Bureau of Prisons.

The Walnut Street Jail, Philadelphia. Courtesy U.S. Bureau of Prisons.

John Haviland — prison architect. Courtesy U.S. Bureau of Prisons.

Sing Sing Prison and the Tappan Zee.

Entire staff of the McNeil Island Territorial Prison about 1880. Courtesy U.S. Bureau of Prisons.

The Tombs in New York.

The Old Capitol Prison, Washington, D.C.

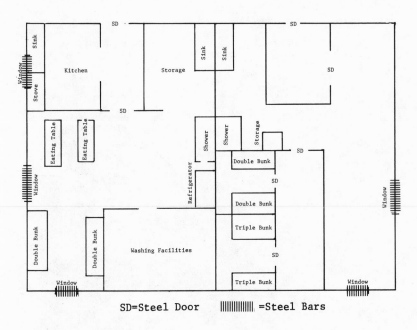

SD=Steel Door ||||||||||||| =Steel Bars

Trusty and Security Section of a small Western county jail, c. 1925.

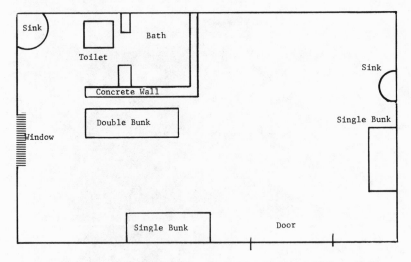

Women and juvenile facility of a small Western county jail, c. 1925.

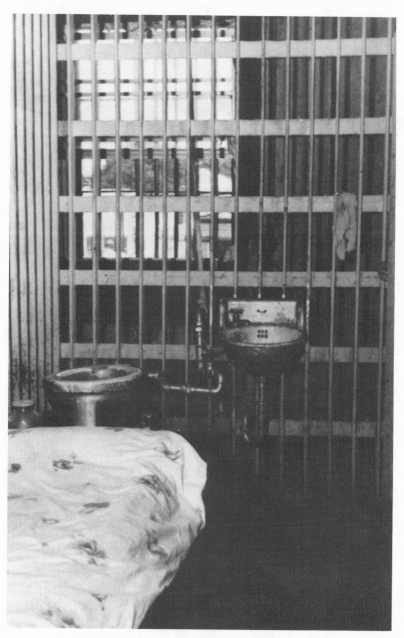

Bad conditions in contemporary American jails.
Courtesy U.S. Bureau of Prisons.

Metropolitan Correctional Center, New York City. This complex has the courts and jails in close proximity. Courtesy U.S. Bureau of Prisons.

An additional description accompanied the letter along with a diagram of the facility (see Appendix A, "New County Prison, Hartford, Connecticut, 1837"). This diagram along with Smith's letter gives us one of the most complete architectural accounts of a jail in that period.

County jails in Ohio were briefly surveyed in a letter written November 20, 1840, by three Ohio residents. As indicated by this letter, the variation between the different geographical areas was great.

> Gentlemen:—I have endeavored to carry into execution the plan you suggested, of visiting such of the County Jails of Ohio as fell within my ride. I have examined the Prisons of twenty-three counties, and have made the inquiries relating to their management, which were permitted by the time I could command, and by my inexperience. I have preserved rough plans of these places of confinement, and notes of the several matters which fell under my observation.
>
> My present object is to communicate the results; for the details, at present, would be of little use. It is strange that the condition of our County Prisons has attracted so little the notice of benevolent men. Most other fields of philanthropy have been more or less explored; our Penitentiary system has been remodeled and reformed, so as nearly to meet the expectations of its friends; but our Common Jails have almost escaped the eyes of Christian charity, and the members of our faith have mostly forgotten the promises of our Master to those who visit the prisoner in Prison. Yet the number of persons in confinement is not too inconsiderable to deserve notice. In the 23 counties, it amounts to 383 persons accused of crime during the past year, and the aggregate time spent is 1301 weeks. Nor is it because there is no need of good officers; for I have been informed, that lately, in one of our principal towns, a respectable stranger, arrested for debt, was enclosed, for several days, in the same cell with an insane black woman; and I have seen the unwashed blanket, which wrapped the limbs of a prisoner, while recovering from exposure in an attempt to escape two years ago, retained in ordinary prison use, of which more than a square yard was stiffened with blood and corrupted matter; and I have heard and believe, that, not many years since, the feet of another were frozen while in confinement in his cell, in spite of his efforts to preserve them.
>
> Since the last law relating to imprisonment for debt, the number of debtors in Jail has become very small. Our penal

system does not rely much upon imprisonment as a punishment, and confinements for this purpose are not numerous. The prisoners in our County Jails are mostly untried criminals. The only demands of society upon these are for safe-keeping. They ought to be subjected to no harshness or restrictions, except those necessary to this object; and they are entitled to wholesome food, pure air, exercise, and other means for the preservation of health, and to the ordinary accommodations and conveniences which tend to mitigate the sufferings of confinement, and are not inconsistent with secure custody.

In all the counties of our state, except Hamilton and Cuyahoga, the number of prisoners rarely exceeds two or three at a time, and the rules applicable to large Prisons, as to separation, &c., are hardly applicable. With the Jail of Hamilton county I am not acquainted. The average number confined in the Cleveland Prison is 14; but the accumulation at each term of the court is considerable. These are distributed in three cells, each about 10 feet by 15, and two rooms above, each about 18 feet square. The rooms are regarded somewhat insecure, and the cells are filled until they will contain no more. The walls of the cells are of squared stone, two feet thick. There is neither window nor fireplace. The aperture of the door-way is closed by two grated doors, which admit the only air, light, or heat, which the apartment receives from without. There are two single bunks below, and two double ones above, filled with loose straw, changed about once in two months. There are no beds. Blankets are used in the bunks, benches for seats, and a large tub, emptied when full, or about once a week. The upper rooms are provided with vaults, which are offensive, except when cleansed by rain. This Jail is kept as cleanly and as well as its construction admits, but it is a grossly improper place of confinement. It is unhealthy from its crowded condition and the impossibility of ventilation. It is so dark, that when the cell door is closed, reading would be difficult in the outer, and impossible in the centre cell; and it admits of no separation of prisoners, of young and old, the hardened and the novice. The people of that county should never rest until these evils are cured.

The other County Jails may be divided into two classes—those provided by the newly-organized counties, as temporary, designed to serve until the finances of the county admit a larger expenditure, and those intended to be permanent. Among the counties I have visited, 9 are of the first, and 14 of the last class. The temporary Jails are built of squared logs, generally unplastered, heated by stoves, and rarely provided with a yard; the large rooms cold, the small, ill ventilated and unhealthy; and the whole insecure, without the use of fetters.

A description of one of this class will answer as a specimen:—

No. 10—built about 15 years ago. It is a log building, 24 feet square, two stories high, standing alone in a lot, without a yard. The lower story is made of two thicknesses of logs, each a foot square, with an interval between them of six inches, filled with stones. The outside door is double, and opens into a lobby 8 feet wide, extending across the whole front of 24 feet. Opposite to the outside door is the door of the first cell, which occupies half the remaining space, or 16 feet by 9. This cell is lighted and ventilated by a diamond in the door, 6 inches square, and by a window in the side, 10 inches by 8, before which stand a few palisades, which exclude all view without. The two walls have settled unequally, so that the opening for the window in one does not correspond with the opening in the other wall, and little light can penetrate. I think a person could not read in this cell, unless by the diamond while the outer door was open. Within this first cell, a close door opens to the second cell, of the same size, but having no light except what shines through a circular window. In the second story is a large room, above these cells, 16 feet by 24, with two grated and sashed windows, and a stove; but the open cracks above and beneath, and on every side, forbid all hope of a comfortable temperature in cold weather. There is another small room above, from the end of the lobby, 6 feet by 6, with a bed on the floor, and no light except what streams through the chinking. In the room upstairs is a bed, a coarse bedstead, and some chairs: below there is no furniture, except a bed on the floor, and a broken door. This Jail has been often broken, and fetters are constantly used, there being no safety without, and little with them.

I will describe a Jail of a more permanent kind:—

No. 17—a well-constructed house, built of brick, except the lower story of the Jail side is of cut stone. The north half is devoted to prisoners, and is separated from the family apartments by a passage through the house. In the centre of the passage, a double door, one grated and one close, opens to another passage, 18 feet long and 5 feet wide, which gives access to four cells, two on each side, each 12 feet by 9. Each cell has a window about seven feet from the floor, large enough to admit three panes of 7 by 9 glass. Each cell has a stove, and a straw bed on a bedstead made by stretching coarse canvass on a frame, and laying it in trestles. The division in the second story is similar, except that each cell contains a common-sized grated window. The whole interior is whitewashed, and looks cleanly. The only fault I discover in its construction is, the absence of a yard, and the want of ventilation in its lower story.

I believe there is no reason for complaint of the food of prisoners, at any of our County Jails in this state. It is ordinarily furnished from the table of the jailer, and in most cases thrice a day.

A considerable difference is found in our Jails, as to personal cleanliness. In most cases, water for washing, and a towel, are provided every morning, and shaving and changing of linen once a week. In most cases, the weekly washing of clothes is done in the jailer's family, without additional charge; but in some counties, such a charge is paid by the county. I believe that necessary clothing and medical attendance for destitute prisoners are provided by the county. But I find in some counties, that no regard is paid by the jailer to the weekly change of clothing. In one county, the jailer informed me he did not furnish water for daily ablutions, because the statute did not direct it to be done.

It is the general usage of our county jailers to admit the counsel of the prisoners at all reasonable times, without restraint; and to permit the visits of prisoners' friends, at convenient times, in the presence of the jailer.

The interests of humanity must excuse plain speaking upon another subject. Various means are adopted of providing for the prisoners' necessities. In a few of the permanent Jails are vaults within the house. I am informed the use of these is abandoned in the best-constructed Prisons, from the difficulty of suppressing bad smells, and preserving them clean without chloride of lime, or other precautions not likely to be used. In some of our Jails, large tubs are employed, and emptied when full; these infect the whole house, and are always objectionable. In others, smaller vessels, sometimes covered, and sometimes open, and daily cleaned. There is much room for reform in this respect, by providing a night-bucket for each prisoner, partly filled with water, to be emptied by him daily, or oftener.

The ordinary use of fetters, as a security from escape, is general in the poorer Jails, and not unfrequent in all. They may be permitted to enforce the observance of Prison rules, and perhaps in some extraordinary cases; but to subject all persons to their annoyance, adds greatly and unnecessarily to the evils of confinement.

There is not much *complaint* of vermin, yet traces of them are found in most of them. In the old log Jails, bed-bugs seem to be the natural inhabitants; fleas are found in most places; and in one I heard of lice. Most of the permanent Jails, however, are washed and scrubbed at convenient intervals, and kept in tolerable tidiness. There is no regular whitewashing; in most cases it is neglected too much; some have been left without this means of purification for a dozen years. No one reform is more needed than a law requiring it, at least twice a year.

I believe that, in none of our County Prisons, lights are furnished in the evening, unless at the expense of the prisoner.

The beds are filled with straw; sheets are not usual; beds are found in about half the Jails.

In the 23 Jails I have visited, I found Bibles in five only. In four of them, I find that books, tracts, and newspapers are provided, with some degree of system; and in some others, their keepers have assured me, that such would be furnished, if asked for. In seven only have I found that clergymen and religious people have visited prisoners. When capital offenses are committed, the clergy of the neighborhood, especially of the denomination in which the criminal has been educated, usually give their attention; in other cases, the prisoner is left to himself.

I cannot refrain from again expressing my surprise at the neglect of this benevolence by good men. The opportunity of rendering a thousand good offices to the destitute,—the rapturous delight and earnest gratitude with which the prisoner accepts every thing which diversifies the monotony of confinement,—would be a rich reward for the trouble. But humanity demands that the community should maintain such an oversight of the Prison-house as will insure to the destitute a supply for his common wants, and prevent the infliction of unnecessary suffering, and repress the disposition, which unwatched men often feel, to tyrannize over those within their power. Besides, Christian duty rarely presents itself in a more pressing form; for the poor outcast, friendless and humiliated, frequently possesses susceptibilities which may be ripened into permanent reform; and the youthful offender, or the novice in crime, may be restored to society a good man, under judicious Christian effort.

You ask me to name such evils as I conceive admit of correction. I have so little knowledge or experience upon this subject, that I cannot rely much upon any plan of reform which

I can frame. At the risk of being deemed officious, I will venture to propose,—

1st. That the commissioners be required to provide, in each county, a Prison, safe without the use of fetters; capable of being warmed and ventilated; large enough to admit classification, by separating young from old, the untried from the convict, with a yard, to prevent unauthorized visits, and to admit some degree of exercise.

2d. That the legislature frame (or cause to be prepared) a plan of treatment of prisoners in County Jails, embracing the points of food, drink, clothing, and medicine, for the destitute, and all matters relating to cleanliness and internal management.

3d. That the grand jury of each county, at each term of the court, be required to visit the Jail.

If a good design of a Prison-house, embracing modern improvements, and costing betweeen $6,000 and $10,000, could be prepared, I think it would be often adopted in our counties.

Our County Jails are likewise used as places of confinement for the insane. I find, in seven counties, 18 insane persons have been kept during this year, whose collective time is 107 weeks. It is hoped that the State Lunatic Asylum will soon be in readiness to receive all such patients; for they can receive no proper medical aid in Jail, and I fear cruelties are sometimes inflicted upon them, both in neglect, and in more active forms, under the name of correction, such as is little suspected by the public.

With my most earnest wishes for the success of the plan you have undertaken, and my thanks for the opportunity you have given me of contributing to it,

I am, with great respect, your ob't serv't,
E. Lane

Messrs. W. H. Channing,
Jas. H. Perkins,
Cincinnati.[13]

Many reformers had suggested that one of the worst things a prisoner could do was to sit in jail without engaging in any productive activity. A few common jails tried to remedy this situation by putting their inmates to work. Another alternative to work in the jail was to work outside the facility under supervision.

The chain gang tradition began in the first half of the nineteenth-century. Also known as the road gang, it was an alternative to sitting out one's time in a jail cell. Although never widely used in either the North or West, in a number of Southern states ". . . there gradually came into existence what has come to be known as the county chain gang system, under which prisoners under county control are used in the building and repair of the public roads."[14]

In many Southern states there were no state prisons, and those convicted of crimes were sentenced to the county jail. Rather than have the criminal lie idle in jail, he would be sentenced to serve time on the county road gang. The chain gangs had the effect of reducing jail population and were also responsible for producing a considerable number of "separate" penal systems within a state because each county was autonomous in the running of its chain gang.

The inmates were often chained together and taken to the area in which they were to work. Temporary camps would be set up and moved as the work progressed. Such camps were crowded and had poor sanitary conditions. They lacked medical care, clean clothes, and bathing facilities. Food was poor, and a minimum of shelter was provided. The sick and well slept and ate together. It was not uncommon to find a syphilitic inmate working, sleeping, drinking, and eating along with the other men.

It was said that conditions in these camps were as bad as those to be found in the jails if not worse. A man or child sentenced to over five years to one of these road gangs probably would not survive.[15] Complaints about these confinement areas did little to change their operations. It was not until well into the twentieth-century that the conscientious reform voices were strong enough to have an effect.

As the westward movement of the nineteenth-century took place, hundreds of thousands of people emigrated west from both Europe and the older regions of the United States. This movement involved not only the good, upstanding citizens and immigrants but also those who had violated the law and would do so again. As need for law and order developed, so did the need to confine offenders; the jail also moved "out west." Wherever enough customers warranted a confinement facility, one was built. Many jails that are shown in

Western movies are not unlike those actually in existence in the West after the Civil War. Some of these structures are still in use, while others are in renovated "Western" towns, and the remains of a few still stand in scattered ghost towns. They were unusually simple in architectural design, adding little if anything to the advancement of jail design. They ranged in size from those holding one or two people to those accommodating thirty or more.

Midwestern jails were about the same as those later found in the far west. The Danville, Illinois, jail, built after the mid-part of the century, was described in the following manner: "The south section of the first floor is a small, dark room containing a cage of five cells and a narrow corridor. The cage and the cell door are built of closely set bars. The cage corridor extends the length of the cells. The cells are of solid iron and are placed back to back with the cells of the north section."[16] The author of the previous quotation, Joseph Fishman, went on to say that the cells were so dark that, while standing in the corridor, one could not see into them. Some of them had cots while others did not, and the inmate was forced to sleep on the floor. When the jail was near capacity, three men were placed in each cell.[17]

Most cells found in jails of this time were about four feet wide by seven feet long by seven feet high.[18] These were very small areas, especially if two or three inmates had to live in them. The men and women so confined had little or nothing to do, and consequently, homosexuality ran rampant; Midwest and Western jails were no exception.

Western jails were administered by an assortment of sheriffs, marshalls, constables, and chiefs of police. Who the chief administrator was depended upon what level of government was involved. In some areas there were towns with sufficient populations to warrant a jail, and a marshall, constable, or chief of police would be in charge of the facility. In other areas the county would develop the jail under the sheriff and would house individuals from different areas within the county. In any case the chief administrator might designate an employee to operate the jail on his behalf.

Jails usually functioned to confine individuals before trial, or to confine those serving sentences on less serious offenses. Some committing less serious offenses were not actually confined. If they were not local residents they might be escorted to the edge of town or the county line and warned not to return. Those convicted of more serious offenses were usually sent to state or territorial prison, if one was available. In some areas the first confinement facilities were built as territorial jails and then turned over to the city or county as the area became a state.

Probably the first jail in Spokane, Washington, was a log structure constructed around 1877. Until 1884, when Joel Warren, the first town marshall, took office and also took charge of the jail, it was used as a territorial jail.[19] A new Spokane jail was built for the city in 1888. In Spokane, the *Morning Review* newspaper said of this facility:

> Chief Warren's boarding house on Riverside Avenue is completed, and will be open for the reception of guests after today.... the building is a very suitable one for prison purposes. It has five cells, including the cage and iron cell for desperate characters or insane persons. The iron cage where the tramps will hold their meetings and recount their sad experiences, is the same one used in the old county jail at Cheney. There is an apartment for females....[20]

The first county jail, constructed in Spokane in 1895, was considered a modern structure. It was five stories high and could house 135 inmates. Its four-man cells, each measuring six feet by eight feet by eight feet, were constructed of steel for maximum security purposes. However, the steel proved to be soft and vulnerable, eventually rusting. This rusting material created very unsanitary conditions.

The history of local jails has become an interesting topic for study. With the widespread contemporary interest in confinement facilities, many local historians and researchers are beginning to produce accounts of these early facilities. The picture of American jails will be more complete once hundreds of these studies are concluded. An example of one of these investigations is the brief history of the nineteenth-century development of the jail in our nation's capital (see Appendix B, A Brief History of the Jails in the District of Columbia).

Internal structures of these early jails did vary somewhat, depending largely upon the geographical location as well as the population of the community served. One innovation of internal confinement was apparently short-lived but nevertheless both interesting and ingenious. It was called the "rotary jail" or "squirrel cage." This cage was constructed so as to sit within a large brick building that had barred windows. The cells were within a permanent steel-barred cylinder that had an opening on each floor. Within that was another revolving steel cylinder, also barred, divided into ten tiny pie-shaped cells, each seven by six feet. Each cell had an opening but no actual door. As the cylinder was revolved, the cell opening and permanent opening coincided and formed an exit, which was secured by a huge, weighted, barred brace. If this was not secure enough the jailer could keep the whole cylinder revolving all night so that the inmate could not saw his way out. A man might go to sleep facing west, be rotated many times and wake up facing east.[21] This type of facility never became popular and was abandoned for more conventional methods of confinement.

Most nineteenth-century jails did not have matrons. While women inmates were segregated in many cases, they were supervised by male jailers. In some cases, women, often the jailers' wives, acted as supervisors. The women's quarters in most jails were probably better than those of the men.

In addition to the segregation of men and women there was also a separation of races, a practice by no means common to all jails but particularly prevalent in the South. Thus, blacks and whites were separated in confinement—both receiving poor treatment. The equality of treatment may not have been a reality, for there is good reason to believe that blacks consistently were treated more harshly than whites. Information regarding this practice is fragmentary and scattered, but there are recorded instances in which white jailers were relieved from duty because of excessive cruelty to black inmates.[22] And no doubt there were many instances in which they were *not* removed.

In some areas two institutions were built side by side, such as those in Albany, New York. One was the Albany County Penitentiary, the other the Albany County Jail. Both facilities actually functioned as jails but in slightly different ways. In the penitentiary were individuals serving sentences from three months to one year.

In the jail were those awaiting trial or serving sentences of less than three months.

The Albany facilities were built in 1847. All cells were alike, measuring eight feet long, four feet wide, and seven feet high, with barred doors two feet wide and little or no light. Each was furnished with two-foot-wide cots and had a bucket for the toilet. They were poorly vented, and bedding was rarely changed.

Jailers of this period appear to have accepted little or no responsibility for the physical condition or cleanliness of their jails, an attitude that persists among many today. Consequently, most were maintained in very poor condition. As in the Albany institutions, many jails lacked sanitary conditions. Inmates used buckets for toilets and were without bathing facilities. Few institutions had the means to prepare food; so it was brought from outside and served on trays. Usually two meals were served daily, with little variation in content.

The poor conditions of many nineteenth-century jails in America were generally acknowledged. Concern for this state of affairs was voiced by scattered groups across the country, but these groups were not able to effect a great deal of change. By and large their condemnations fell on unconcerned and unsympathetic ears. The reform advocates of the previous century *had* been able to generate change in that laws were altered and new facilities built to house long-term offenders. But jails were not the focal concern of these efforts.

Charity boards existed in many states. They made inspections and annual reports, but their impact on jail conditions was minimal.[23] This may have been due, not only to lack of interest on the part of the citizenry, but also to the fact that the county jails and town lockups were under local control and not subject to state regulations. This situation is still prevalent in many states.

The quotation that follows, from the First Annual Report of the Illinois State Charities Commission in 1910, was a repeat of similar findings in the latter part of the nineteenth-century: "Waste, extravagance, inhumanity, inefficiency, neglect, indifference, petty partisan and factional politics making gains of unfortunates; the jails, schools for crime; . . . these were found in 1870 by the State

Board of Charity; these were found in 1910 by the State Charities Commission."

What was the status of jails and prisons as the nineteenth-century ended? The pentitentiary system that began early in the century was well developed in most states. Notable exceptions were in some of the Southern states. New jails had been constructed, particularly in the West where the population was increasing. There continued to be a lack of concern by most citizens with regard to conditions of imprisonment. Exceptions were some private social agencies and the members of a few public boards that undertook to investigate jail conditions. It was these who laid the groundwork for many of the great changes that would occur in twentieth-century American jails.

7

Jails of the Twentieth Century

The jails of the early twentieth century represent a heterogeneous group of institutions. There was no typical jail, nor is there one even now. They varied in size from those with only one or two individuals to complexes of jails that held several thousand people. Some had better facilities than others, and some were better conducted than others.

As the United States moved into the twentieth century, changes were beginning to affect the jails. These changes were occurring primarily with regard to conditions and were originating from sources outside as well as inside the facility. One source of change was the state legislature. For example, just before the turn of the century the state of Minnesota passed an act that had an effect upon the jails of that state. The General Laws of 1895, Chapter 263, read:

> To Regulate the Construction and Management of
> City and Village Lockups
> Be it enacted by the Legislature of the State of Minnesota:
> *Section 1.* The common council of any incorporated city or
> legally organized village in the State of Minnesota is hereby
> authorized and empowered to purchase, build or lease and
> maintain and regulate one or more lockups for the detention of
> persons charged with offenses against the ordinances or by-laws
> of said city or village, or for the confinement of persons
> sentenced to imprisonment for the violation of such ordinances

and by-laws. It shall also be lawful, under such regulations such as council may prescribe, to use such lockup for the temporary detention of any prisoner arrested under due process of law.

Sec. 2. It shall be unlawful for any city or village council to lease or purchase or to make final adoption of plans for the building of any lockup or for repairs costing more than one hundred ($100) dollars, until the plans of said lockup or said repairs shall have been approved by the State Board of Corrections and Charities; and no contract for the purchase or lease or erection of any city or village lockup shall be valid or of binding effect unless the suggestions and criticisms of the said Board of Corrections and Charities shall have been placed on file in the office of the city clerk or the village recorder, as the case may be, before the execution of said contract.

Sec. 3. It shall be unlawful for the State Board of Corrections and Charities to approve any plan for a village lockup unless the said lockup shall contain at least two separate rooms and unless it is to be constructed of fireproof material, or is to have all woodwork, within and without the building, except window frames and window sash, thoroughly covered with tin, sheet iron or other fireproof material.

Sec. 4. It shall be the duty of the chief of police or the village marshal, as the case may be, to see that the lockup and the bedding therein is kept at all times clean, wholesome and free from vermin. It shall be his duty to cause the lockup to be swept daily and thoroughly cleansed with water at least once in two weeks, unless it is unoccupied.

Sec. 5. It shall be unlawful to keep male and female prisoners in the same room, or to keep insane persons or children under sixteen (16) years of age in the same room with other prisoners. So far as practicable, each prisoner in the lockup shall be kept in a separate cell.

Sec. 6. It shall be the duty of the chief of police or the village marshal, as the case may be, to keep a true and exact register of all prisoners committed to the lockup, and all persons admitted to the lockup as lodgers, in such form as the State Board of Corrections and Charities may prescribe; and the same shall be kept in a book to be provided by the city or village.

Sec. 7 It shall be the duty of the mayor of every city or village in which such lockup is located to appoint some discreet and competent woman of good character as matron for each lockup located in said city or village, who shall have exclusive charge of all women committed to such lockup, and shall receive such compensation as the said common council from time to time determines, not less than fifty (50) cents for each day when there are female prisoners confined in the lockup.

Sec. 8. No officer in charge of any lockup shall deliver or permit any other person to deliver to any inmate of such lockup any spirituous liquor, or any mixed liquor, part of which is spirituous, or any wine, cider, or beer, unless a physician shall certify in writing that the health of such prisoner requires it, in which case he may be allowed the quantity prescribed and no more.

Sec. 9. It shall be the duty of the health officer of every city and village to inspect the lockup once in each year of his official term with reference to its sanitary condition, to make a written report of his inspection to the State Board of Corrections and Charities on such blanks as said board shall prescribe and to present a copy of said report to the city or village council; and said health officer shall receive from the treasury of said city or village the sum of two ($2) dollars for every such annual inspection; provided, that the said fee shall not be paid until he shall have first filed his report as aforesaid.

Sec. 10. Any officer neglecting the duties prescribed in sections four (4), five (5), six (6), eight (8) and nine (9) of this act shall be guilty of a misdemeanor;

Sec. 11. All acts and parts of acts inconsistent with this act are hereby repealed.

Sec. 12. This act shall take effect and be in force from and after its passage.

Unfortunately, not all states passed legislation of this type, and in many instances when it was passed, there was little or no enforcement authority. This is common today. Many states have laws pertaining to their jails but no agency to enforce the laws.

There was another sort of change taking place in this country at the turn of the century: the growth of the city. The urban movement, which began to expand in the last part of the preceding century, was well under way. It had its effect upon jails in that more people were concentrated in smaller areas and in larger population units. Crime increased; more and larger confinement facilities were required, but few new jails were built, and the existing ones were simply packed with more inmates.

Most jails in operation at the beginning of the century were very old and in need of replacement. Many were, in fact, over 100 years old, although they may have undergone changes in name and governing authority. Some workhouses had become state institutions, such as those in Massachusetts. In other places workhouses were maintained and operated by a town, city or county. In some locations the workhouse was an annex, leaving the jail for untried prisoners. In other places the workhouse was the city prison. The original hodgepodge of titles and functions thus continued into this century. To add to the already existing variations, authorities in various parts of the country held untried persons in stockades. In other areas the untried were confined to houses of correction. Confinement policies and practices across the country were diverse.

Also persisting into this century was the turnkey fee—the fee paid the jailer when the inmate was either locked up or released. Another related source of income for a jailer was the "savings" he was able to make from the money paid for feeding the inmates. The older system that charged the inmate for his own food had generally disappeared and was being replaced by money allotted for food by the local or state government.

The sheriff, for example, was paid a certain amount depending upon the number of inmates he had in his facility. After he fed the inmates, any funds left over would go into his pocket. In some states jailers were prone to raise dietary fees as counties improved their financial position. Consequently fees paid the sheriff may have been increased, but he was not necessarily compelled to use the money for additional food. Table 7.1 is based upon a study completed in 1933 that showed the amount paid sheriffs for feeding prisoners in the state of Georgia.

Table 7.1 **The Amount Paid Sheriffs for Feeding Inmates in the State of Georgia During the Year 1933**

Amount per Day per Inmate	Number of Counties Paying Such Amount
$ 1.00	1
.80	1
.75	15
.70	3
.65	11
.60	42
.55	7
.50	53
.45	9
.40	8
weighted average $ .567	total counties 150

From this study it can be seen that there were tremendous differences among the counties as to the amount they paid their sheriffs to feed inmates. County officials also expected these fees to be used for other items in addition to food. Therefore, out of the fees came (1) the cost of preparing the food, (2) the cost of paying the guards, and (3) other operating expenses.

Financing the operations of jails had always been a problem and continued as one into the twentieth century. Although there was a variety of methods of financing in the different states, one common element in all of them was the fact that they were underfinanced. There just never seemed to be enough money to operate jails as they should be operated. While some of these facilities were in better financial condition than others, Southern states continued to maintain jails with the lowest budgets.

Sometime during the development of American confinement institutions, a clear distinction occurred between the jail and the lockup. The lockup (sometimes referred to as the police lockup) is a municipal institution that is generally administered by the city police. Held in lockups are usually those confined for less than forty-eight hours and quite often those charged with offenses to be heard in lower courts. These lockups differ from either the county or city jails, which hold all classes of people and may detain them for long periods of time.

Lockups, as a rule, are found in larger cities and generally serve specific areas of a city. Thus a large city may have several lockups, one in each of its districts or precincts. Some small towns may have lockups administered by local enforcement officers for holding the less seriously charged offenders and may transport their serious offenders to the county jail.

Most lockups have never been particularly good places to hold people. They are still used and in many cases have not improved. A 1910 description is close to what one would find today in some of them.

> In many of the crowded station houses little care is taken to classify prisoners. Decent men are made cellmates with the vilest; men who are cleanly in person and in clothing are put with the filthy and verminous. Drinking cups and food dishes, used indiscriminately by all sorts of prisoners, are rarely if ever

sterilized. All these things are especially dangerous, because many of the prisoners are diseased in various ways and many others are so lacking in vitality as to be an easy prey to contagious and infectious diseases.[1]

At the beginning of the century, jails in the United States were not much better than they had been during the preceding century. There were some scattered exceptions, mainly the newly constructed ones. Jail reform movements that were operating in the last century became more vocal, and literature on the subject increased. Both emphasized the continued poor conditions of the jails.

Fishman repeats the vivid picture of South Carolina jails in the first part of this century given by the South Carolina State Board of Public Welfare. Here is what was said about jails in some of the counties:

Abbeville County: The cells are dark and poorly ventilated. The prisoners' quarters have only one bath tub and one toilet. Each cell consequently has to have a refuse bucket as well as a bucket of drinking water, both of them constantly exposed to flies, since the upper floors of the building are not screened.

Aiken County: Badly in need of repairs. The roof leaks. In rainy weather the water pours down into the jail in torrents. Plumbing in poor shape, bath tubs useless, and toilets can only be flushed with difficulty.

Bamberg County: Sewage not properly disposed of. Soil buckets emptied in a hole about 75 yards from the building, but no dirt thrown on it. Flies swarming around.

Beaufort County: Food lacking in variety and wholesomeness. Floor and bedding dirty.

Calhoun County: Lack of facilities results in all the prisoners being herded into one room—*men, women and children.*

Chester County: Scraps of food lying around. Drain pipes from combination drinking fountains and lavatories stopped up with refuse. Bedding and jail dirty.

Cherokee County: Dirty. Dog sleeping on extra pile of blankets. Insufficient food.

Chesterfield: Panes of glass out of windows. Jail improperly heated.

Clarendon County: Cell block needed thorough cleaning, scraps of decaying food lying around. Improperly heated.

Colleton County: Plumbing in deplorable condition. Pipes

leak so badly water can be turned on only once a day, when a supply must be caught for drinking, laundering, cooking, bathing, and for flushing the sewerage system. Dirty, no bathing rules, and generally unfit.

Darlington County: Heating arrangements inadequate. Cells dark.

Dillon County: In deplorable condition. Defective plumbing. Lower floor of jail had recently been covered with several inches of water. *Jailer's family stated that at this time a negro convict died in the jail of influenza, and the water under his cot was over an inch deep on the night of his death.*

Fairfield County: Floor cannot be scoured because water runs through cracks into sheriff's home below. Building fire trap. Bedding dirty.

Georgetown County: Bath tub for negroes out of commission, and galvanized tubs used instead. Drain pipe of tub for white prisoners clogged so that the water must be emptied by dipping most of the dirty water from it with a pail. Toilets almost beyond use from lack of repairs, and one of them leaking badly.

Lancaster County: Cells veritable wooden dungeons, with no windows, the only light and air coming through small heavily barred doors. *Even with the cell door wide open the cell is so dark that an inmate cannot see the ceiling clearly enough to tell of what material it is built.* Not one ray of sunlight ever penetrates this house of darkness that is so much better adapted for the habitation of bats and owls than of human beings.

Laurens County: Living conditions extremely unsatisfactory. Toilets out of order and fill building with bad odors. Heating so unsatisfactory that colored men sleep on floor in order to be near stove. Bath tubs useless from lack of repairs. Supply of blankets so scanty that none can be spared during the cold months for the laundry. Men, both white and colored, sleeping under covering that is so soiled that it is positively filthy. Whole building dark and dirty.

Lexington County: Sanitary arrangements miserable. No hot water for bathing. *No stove or other heating facilities at all.* Prisoners suffering with cold so that they used tin tub for stove by filling it with chips and trash. Smoke filled room. But in addition to no heating facilities, *several of the window panes are broken.*

Marion County: Bedding unsatisfactory and generally filthy. Men sleep on pallets on the floor.

Marlboro County: The building has only two compartments, making it almost impossible to separate properly the prisoners according to *sex*, race and age.[2]

In a general report H. H. Hart says there were many defects among the jails and lockups of the first part of this century (see Appendix C, Police Jails and Village Lockups). He cites nine glaring ones:

First, many are located in city halls, village buildings, or fire stations, where they occupy space needed for other purposes, and where dirty, noisy, and drunken prisoners are brought into close proximity with public officers and visitors.

Second, some lockups are in separate buildings, on the city hall square, necessitating architecture conforming to that of the city hall, while others are located on eligible and expensive corner lots requiring too expensive architectural faces.

Third, thousands of police jails and lockups are firetraps and not infrequently prisoners have been cremated in them.

Fourth, many lockups are antiquated buildings unfit for the purpose. Perhaps all of these old lockups are unsanitary, without adequate lighting, heating, ventilation, or plumbing.

Fifth, very few lockups make proper provision for the segregation and classification of women, witnesses, and young people.

Sixth, many lockups in small cities and villages are used also as lodging places for tramps and vagrants. These lodgers who may be dirty and verminous make it almost impossible to keep the lockup clean and sanitary.

Seventh, very few lockups are properly furnished. Usually the prisoners sleep on wooden or iron bunks, generally without mattresses or blankets. If blankets or mattresses are provided, they are seldom kept clean and the bunks are often verminous.

Eighth, the "third degree" is practiced extensively throughout the United States, with cruel and illegal treatment and sometimes torture of persons accused of crime, whether innocent or guilty.

Ninth, there is a lack of state supervision of lockups. County jails may have state inspection but police jails and lockups generally are left to the caprice and indifference of local officials and citizens of cities and villages where even clergy and social workers pay little or no attention.[3]

The above comments on jails in general and the description of the South Carolina jails are typical of those published earlier this century. In addition to noting the deficiencies several writers also make recommendations to correct them.[4] An example of these recommendations is that by H. H. Hart.

1. Provide for at least six classifications in every police jail to separate males and females, old and young, sick and well, dangerous and harmless classes.

2. Keep each prisoner in a separate cell and abolish the practice of doubling up prisoners or confining 6, 8, or 10 in a single cell.

3. Every police jail or lockup should be strictly fireproof.

4. Women prisoners in the hands of the police should be kept absolutely separate from male prisoners where communication would be impossible.

5. Legislation should be adopted to abolish the illegal and unregulated practice of the "third degree" by policemen and detectives.

6. In every state provision should be made by law for the supervision and inspection of police stations by a responsible State commission, with power to condemn buildings unfit for use, in accordance with the longstanding practice in the States of New York and Minnesota.

7. The personnel of jailers, guards, and matrons in police lockups should be radically improved.

8. Police jails and lockups should be intelligently planned by competent architects.[5]

These comments and suggestions were written by Hart during the first part of the 1930s. Similar comments had been voiced by scattered groups and individuals for some two hundred years preceding that date. Although most of these observations fell on deaf ears, some people listened. A great deal of documentation on the state of jails became available and, consequently, the recommendations have been acted upon by different authorities in the United States.

In response to conditions found in many jails as well as the need to provide direction to jailers, the National Sheriffs' Association developed a series of standards. Although compulsory enforcement is impossible, compliance with these standards is recommended by the association (see Appendix D, Jail Standards of the National Sheriffs' Association).

During the twentieth century the jailers themselves began to take an interest in their collective occupation, their working conditions, and to a lesser degree, the conditions of their jails, resulting in the National Jailers Association being organized in the early twentieth century. Although most of the nation's jails were not represented in the organization, it began to develop a forum to consider many of the problems of jails, jailers, and inmates.

In 1974 the Jail Managers Association came into being, and, although it is quite small, it too provides a discussion forum for the many problems facing management of jails as well as jail employees. Neither the National Jail Association nor the Jail Managers Association is *the* organization to represent jails and jailers on a national level, for neither has a large membership. It may be that no such organization will emerge until much later.

In the past few years, several states have developed their own jailers' associations.[6] In some instances these have been effective organizations in lobbying for jails and jailers, but in other instances they have not. The development should be seen as a move toward professionalism.

Training for jailers has also become an important ingredient in progress toward professionalism. During the 1960s and 1970s there has been an effort, often with support from the federal government, in this direction. Before this, jailers were trained chiefly on the job, which in most cases merely taught the officer how to handle himself and the inmates. Training often consisted of showing him how to (1) handle keys, (2) use force in dealing with inmates, and (3) protect himself from harm. There was very little systematic instruction in such areas as psychology, sociology, management, and budgeting.

Several cities, counties, and states now present training courses for their jailers; even if sponsored by the state, these courses are taught on local levels. The state of Washington, for example, offers courses through the Washington State Criminal Justice Training Commission. Each is eighty hours in duration, and they are presented in different locations throughout the state.[7]

Table 7.2 outlines the basic course taught in Washington State. Special note should be made of the variety of topics presented. Different instructors are brought in so as to expose the student to a number of individuals who have expertise in several areas. The jailers have a voice in the content of their course, and so the outline reflects some of the contemporary jail problems and situations that concern them. Most courses include coverage of law, noncriminal deviant behavior, and security (see Appendix E, Course Outline: Abnormal Behavior in the Jail).

In addition to this basic course, jailers are also offered three-day minicourses presented in various locations. Topics offered in these short courses may vary from year to year.

Table 7.2

Basic Training Course for Jailers
Washington State Criminal Justice Training Commission
Corrections Officers Academy 203 A-E
Class Schedule

Monday
8:00 A.M. – 9:00 A.M.	Preliminaries; Pretest
9:00 A.M. – 10:30 A.M.	Opening Remarks
10:30 A.M. – 11:00 A.M.	Overview—Program Goals
11:00 A.M. – 12:00 noon	Criminal Justice Systems
12:00 noon – 1:00 P.M.	Lunch
1:00 P.M. – 3:00 P.M.	Criminal Justice Systems
3:00 P.M. – 4:00 P.M.	Professional Journals—Selected Articles
4:00 P.M. – 5:00 P.M.	Institutions

Tuesday
8:00 A.M. – 11:00 A.M.	Systems and Institutions in Turmoil
11:00 A.M. – 12:00 noon	How We Judge People
12:00 noon – 1:00 P.M.	Lunch
1:00 P.M. – 2:00 P.M.	How We Judge People
2:00 P.M. – 4:00 P.M.	Cultural Differences
4:00 P.M. – 5:00 P.M.	Aggressive Behavior, Sexual Deviation and Suicide

Wednesday
8:00 A.M. – 12:00 noon	Interpersonal Relationships
12:00 noon – 1:00 P.M.	Lunch
1:00 P.M. – 5:00 P.M.	Communications

Thursday
8:00 A.M. – 12:00 noon	First Aid—Multimedia System
12:00 noon – 1:00 P.M.	Lunch
1:00 P.M. – 5:00 P.M.	First Aid—Multimedia System

Table 7.2—*Continued*

Friday

8:00 A.M. – 10:00 A.M.	First Aid in an Institutional Setting
10:00 A.M. – 12:00 noon	Institutional Climate—Standards and Goals
12:00 noon – 1:00 P.M.	Lunch
1:00 P.M. – 3:00 P.M.	State of Washington Corrections—Detention Systems
3:00 P.M. – 5:00 P.M.	Just the Keeper of the Keys?

Monday

8:00 A.M. – 10:00 A.M.	Positive Use of Authority
10:00 A.M. – 12:00 noon	Parole Board
12:00 noon – 1:00 P.M.	Lunch
1:00 P.M. – 4:00 P.M.	Classification of Inmates—Jail and Long-Term Institutions
4:00 P.M. – 5:00 P.M.	Role of the Prosecutor

Tuesday

8:00 A.M. – 12:00 noon	Investigation, Evidence and Courtroom Demeanor
12:00 noon – 1:00 P.M.	Lunch
1:00 P.M. – 3:00 P.M.	Community Corrections
3:00 P.M. – 5:00 P.M.	Female—Staff and Inmates

Wednesday

8:00 A.M. – 10:00 A.M.	Receiving and Discharging of Prisoners
10:00 A.M. – 12:00 noon	Ethics
12:00 noon – 1:00 P.M.	Lunch
1:00 P.M. – 3:00 P.M.	Policies, Procedures, and Emergency Plans
3:00 P.M. – 5:00 P.M.	Landmark Decisions, Case Law, Standards and Goals for Corrections

Thursday

8:00 A.M. – 11:00 A.M.	Correctional Counseling
11:00 A.M. – 12:00 noon	Inmate Control, Strip Search, and Contraband
12:00 noon – 1:00 P.M.	Lunch
1:00 P.M. – 2:00 P.M.	Inmate Control—Search, Frisk, and Contraband
2:00 P.M. – 3:00 P.M.	Post Test
3:00 P.M. – 5:00 P.M.	Transportation of Prisoners

Friday

8:00 A.M. – 4:00 P.M.	Tour of Federal Prison, McNeil Island, Washington
4:00 P.M. – 5:00 P.M.	Question-and-Answer Period

Jail problems in the twentieth century are those that have always existed: economic, political, and social problems. They are economic in the sense that there is seldom enough money to operate the jail properly. Employees are low-paid, resulting in failure to attract qualified personnel. Most jails are short of staff, and personnel are overworked. The jails also lack sufficient funds to finance material items as well as treatment programs. Due to underfunding and nonbudgeted expenses, most managers are hard put during the year to make ends meet.

Politically, jails are often used as pawns to be controlled in various ways by local governments. Some communities take pride in being able to say that local authority controls the local jail. Consequently, regardless of the dilapidated condition of their facilities, some cities and counties fight to retain this dubious honor, while the harried administrators of these jails would eagerly shed their frustrating responsibilities of management and control. This jurisdictional autonomy helps to explain the resistance of local governments toward standardized control of jails.

In a social sense there is still little general public concern for the jail, its jailers, or inmates. Facilities in many communities remain poor. People who pass within yards of them daily remain unaware of their condition. Due to certain large events that have brought attention to the prisons, there is some public concern for those institutions, but jails have received little similar attention. The primary notice incurred by jails results from a riot or escape.

The twentieth century saw the appearance of a new location for jails. Instead of being located in a separate building, they were constructed on the top floors of city and county administrative buildings, creating the phenomenon of the high-rise jail. At first this idea was considered very innovative and advanced, but soon problems began to develop. In the earlier types, one of the main difficulties was the transportation of inmates to these top floors. Another problem was that of the mingling of inmates with people who had business to transact not related to the jail.

This type of facility continues to exist, and in fact high-rise jails are still being built. The problem of transportation has generally been solved by the installation of elevators that may be loaded in a secluded area on the main floor or in the basement and go directly to the jail. Inmates need not mingle with those conducting government business if the design of the public buildings is correct. Due to landspace problems faced by many cities and counties, high-rise jails may be a necessity if they are to be located within certain jurisdictions.

In an attempt to resolve some of the economic and political problems associated with jails, there has been a recent trend in the United States to combine city and county jails into one facility. This is presently one of the more innovative plans, and its advantages are many. They include a saving of money, personnel, equipment, time, and effort. The disadvantages are basically the loss of local autonomy.

In cities and counties where these joint jails exist, several administrative models can be identified, but all of the new kind of facility are staffed and operated by one jurisdiction or by both. In cases where one jurisdiction operates the facility, it may control all of the operation and charge the other jurisdiction for holding its inmates. Where the new facility is a joint operation, the sheriff's and police staffs work together in administering the jail; the parent jurisdictions (city council and county commissioners) pool resources and finance the operation.

Some of the combined facilities and, for that matter, those that are not combined, have felt pressure to place control of their jails under a corrections department or similar organization. This arrangement has presented some problems in determining who will be charged with the security of the jail. Many feel it is important to have law-enforcement personnel in this capacity, while others feel that different individuals should be responsible for jailing and administering. Several states are moving toward jails operated by non–law-enforcement personnel. In this event laws usually have to be enacted to remove the sheriff and police chief from their jail obligations. Whether this trend continues or not will be determined with the passing of time.

The function of the jail also seems to be changing in some places in the United States. There is a strong awareness that jails are generally counterproductive to human growth and experience; jailing is seen as a negative experience. Fishman's statement—"Guaranteed Criminal Made in American Jails"—reflects an important insight.[8] Due to a lack of meaningful statistics, we are not sure what the recidivism rate (return rate) is, but it may easily be 70 to 80 percent. That is, seven or eight people out of ten will be returned to jail following the first offense.

In addition to those returning, it must be remembered that most felons spend some time in jails before they begin serving time in a state institution. Incidentally, there is also a trend to have some felons serve their sentences in jail and then be released on early parole. The courts may do this because of poor conditions found in many state prisons. It is questionable in some instances which is worse, the prison or the jail.

The housing of felons in jails is presenting new problems for jailers. Many of these facilities do not offer suitable space or training for serious offenders. Most felons are much more difficult to maintain and handle than the usual inmate.

Some of those who see the jail as having a changing function would like to have it become treatment-oriented, rather than punishment-oriented. Instead of just warehousing people until their release, treatment programs have been initiated. Such programs may not only serve the function of treatment but also help to keep the "lid on" the institution, that is, keep the emotional climate in check. At this time there are few data on the success of treatment in such programs, but there is some indication that certain of them do help in keeping order in the jail.[9]

Example of some jail programs are:

General Programs
  Religious
  Recreational
  Library
  Newspaper
  Arts and Crafts
  Trusty

Counseling and Therapy
  Legal
  General
  Family
  Alcohol
  Drug
  Individual Therapy
  Group Therapy

Educational Programs
  General Equivalency
    Diploma
  College Courses
  Correspondence Courses
  Job Orientation

Other Programs
  Work Release
  Group Living[10]

As we have noted, jails in the twentieth century have undergone considerable change. It was also during this century that the first nationwide jail survey and census took place; it did a great deal to describe conditions and operations of contemporary American jails. As yet the total impact of this survey has not been felt. It is, however, a most important document.

8

National Jail Census and Contemporary Jails

Complete and reliable information on all aspects of jails in the United States has never existed. In fact, even partial information on many American jail characteristics did not exist until the 1970s. At that time, the National Criminal Justice Information and Statistics Service (of the Law Enforcement Assistance Administration, U.S. Department of Justice) entered into an agreement with the United States Bureau of the Census for a national census of jails, to be conducted in the spring of 1970.[1]

The object of this monumental survey was to collect information on the nation's jails and their inmates, on a state-by-state basis.[2] The information sought included the number of jails, the number and types of inmates, the number of persons employed, the cost of operation, and the availability of various selected facilities within jails.[3]

Although the survey did not supply all the data that many would like, it did present a very clear picture of those elements that were surveyed, and its importance cannot be overemphasized. Not since H. H. Hart's attempt in the earlier part of the century has there been such an ambitious and informative project.[4] It is to be hoped that more surveys of this nature will be undertaken. There are numerous items not covered that should be surveyed.

The remainder of this chapter contains verbatim portions of the *National Jail Census, 1970.* (For detailed tables on the findings, see Appendix G, Tables from The National Jail Census.)[5]

Method of Collection

In the spring of 1970, the U.S. Bureau of the Census canvassed each county in the United States and each municipality which had 1960 population of one thousand or more persons to ascertain the presence of a jail. The canvassing included only those jails which are operated locally by the jurisdiction involved; that is, a county, city, or township. State-operated facilities, such as those in Connecticut, Delaware, and Rhode Island, were not included.

Jails surveyed were those which confine inmates for 48 hours or more. Drunk-tanks, lock-ups and similar facilities which normally retain persons for less than two full days were excluded.

An individual facility, such as a jail-farm or annex, which is administratively dependent upon a parent institution, was counted as a separate jail if it is located in a separate geographical area and holds inmates for forty-eight hours or more. Hospitals for the criminally insane and institutions designed for the exclusive use of juveniles were excluded from the jail census.[6]

The jail census was conducted by mail using two different questionnaires. Police chiefs in municipalities of less than twenty-five thousand population were sent questionnaires containing items relating to the composition of the inmate population by type of retention; by sex, and by whether adult or juvenile; designed capacity; retention authority; age of the institution; and employment and expenditure data.[7] County sheriffs and police chiefs in cities of twenty-five thousand population or greater were sent questionnaires containing all the above items and, in addition, questions on the age of the cells and the presence of various kinds of facilities.

Survey questionnaires were mailed in April 1970, with follow-up requests to nonrespondents in May. Where necessary, a telephone callback procedure was employed to obtain missing data. For the major data items, the response rate achieved through these techniques was 100 percent.

General

Jails in the United States confined 160,863 inmates, an average of about 40 inmates each in the 4,037 local jails with forty-eight-hour retention authority. The overwhelming majority of the inmates were adult males—nine out of ten. Others included juveniles as well as adult females—each accounting for about one in twenty of the inmate population. The state of California contained the largest inmate population with 27,672, or 17 per cent of the total. The only other states with more than 10,000 inmates were New York and Texas with 17,399 and 10,720, respectively.

Altogether, however, six states—the three already named plus Florida, Pennsylvania, and Georgia—accounted for 78,829 inmates or about half the total number confined in the United States. These same six states, on the other hand, contained about one-fourth of the U.S. population according to preliminary figures from the 1970 Decennial Census. Vermont, by contrast, had only 22 inmates in its jails on the survey date.

By region, the South had by far the largest number of inmates on March 15—a total of 61,655 (see table 8.1). By comparison, the Northeast and North Central each had only about half as many inmates, 31,458 and 29,209, respectively. There were 38,541 in the West.

Juveniles in Adult Institutions

Every state, except Connecticut, Delaware, and Rhode Island which do not have locally administered jails, contained some adult jails which have the authority to incarcerate juveniles for varying types of retention. On the census date, March 15, there were 7,800 juveniles confined in the 4,037 jails. Over 4,500 juveniles were reported in the state of New York. A large number (3,943) of these, however, were confined in the New York City Reformatory and the New York City Adolescent Remand Shelter. While these inmates are sixteen to twenty-one years old and, therefore, legally adults according to New York State law, they are regarded by New York officials as "youthful offenders." For survey purposes they were classified as juveniles.

Including New York, only twelve states had as many as 100

juveniles confined in their adult jails on March 15. Pennsylvania, Indiana, and Ohio were the only other states with more than 200 juvenile inmates.

Inmates by Type of Retention—Adults and Juveniles

There are four basic categories of retention—sentenced prisoners, convicted persons under appeal or awaiting sentencing, pre-trial detainees, and persons either not yet arraigned or being held for other authorities.[8] The last two groups make up a "not convicted inmate" category, which accounted for just over half (52 percent) of the total inmates in jail. For adult females this percentage was slightly higher at 55 percent. For juveniles the proportion was much higher. Two out of three young people in adult jails were pre-trial detainees or were otherwise not convicted.

Table 8.1 shows regional differences in the proportion of adult and juvenile inmates who had not been convicted of a crime.

There is very little variation by region in the proportion of adult inmates who were not convicted. Only the West region was under half, however, with 46.9 percent. As for juvenile inmates, however, differences vary widely by region and except for the Northeast region the proportion of juvenile inmates not convicted is dramatically higher than the corresponding adult figure. Overall, 66 percent of the juveniles are in the "not convicted" category. For the Northeast, this proportion drops to 54 percent, which is comparable to the 52 percent adult figure for that region. A sharp departure from the Northeast pattern is evident in the other three regions. In the North Central, five out of six juvenile inmates are detained in jail without a conviction; in the South the proportion is about seven out of eight; and in the West it is nine of every ten.

Among the states, the District of Columbia has the lowest percentage (29 percent) of its inmates in the "not convicted" category. This is partly due to the Federal Bail Reform Act of 1966 which is binding on the District of Columbia. This act curtails considerably the use of pre-trial detention and especially money bail.

Of the 27,460 persons being held for other authorities or not yet arraigned, eight states—California, Texas, Florida, Illinois, Ohio, New York, Georgia, and Pennsylvania—account for 15,132, or 55 percent. These same states contain 46 percent of the United States population.

Table 8.1
Number and Percent of Jail Inmate Population Not Convicted, by Age
(Adult or Juvenile) and by Region—March 1970

Region†	Total	Adult Inmates			Juvenile Inmates		
		Total	Not Convicted††	Percentage Not Convicted	Total	Not Convicted††	Percentage Not Convicted
Total, U.S.	160,863	153,063	77,921	50.9	7,800	5,158	66.1
Northeast	31,458	26,526	13,648	51.5	4,932	2,684	54.4
North Central	29,209	28,226	14,654	51.9	983	816	83.0
South	61,655	60,330	31,797	52.7	1,325	1,152	86.9
West	38,541	37,981	17,822	46.9	560	506	90.4

† *Northeast region:* Connecticut, Maine, Massachusetts, New Hampshire, New Jersey, New York, Pennsylvania, Rhode Island, and Vermont. *North Central region:* Illinois, Indiana, Iowa, Kansas, Michigan, Minnesota, Missouri, Nebraska, North Dakota, Ohio, South Dakota, and Wisconsin. *The South:* Alabama, Arkansas, Delaware, Florida, Georgia, Kentucky, Louisiana, Maryland, Mississippi, North Carolina, Oklahoma, South Carolina, Tennessee, Texas, Virginia, West Virginia, and the District of Columbia. *The West:* Alaska, Arizona, California, Colorado, Hawaii, Idaho, Montana, Nevada, New Mexico, Oregon, Utah, Washington, and Wyoming. (*National Jail Census, 1970,* p.7.)
†† Not convicted inmates include persons held for other authorities, those not yet arraigned, and those arraigned and awaiting trial.

Pre-trial detainees were concentrated largely in just six states. California, New York, Texas, Pennsylvania, Florida, and Michigan accounted for over half the total U.S. inmates in this category—29,829 out of 55,619. Likewise, the five states of New York, Texas, Florida, California, and Virginia contained about half—4,461 out of 8,688—the convicted inmates who were awaiting further legal action. New York has more than two and a half times as many persons in this category as the second highest state—Texas.

Of those inmates who are serving sentences, 15 percent are jailed for longer than a year. Altogether, 69,096 persons are serving sentences of varying lengths in the nation's local jails. California has the largest number of sentenced prisoners in its local jails serving one year or less—14,076. Next is New York with 5,309, followed by Florida with 3,821. Those three states together with Michigan, Georgia, and Ohio contribute 30,007—or 51 percent—of the 58,600 prisoners serving sentences of a year or less. Although the District of Columbia, Georgia, Pennsylvania, New York, and South Carolina contain only two out of ten of the nation's citizens, they contain seven out of ten of the local-jail prisoners serving sentences of more than one year.

Facilities Available and Age of Cells

For those jails located either in cities of twenty-five thousand or greater population, or in counties, information was obtained in the census relating to the presence of various facilities, as well as the ages of the cells in the institutions. There are 3,319 jails which are either county-operated or are located in municipalities of twenty-five thousand or more people. For the United States 86 percent of these jails were found to be without facilities for exercise or other recreation. Many states have 95 to 100 percent of their local jails lacking in recreational facilities. Fourteen of 18 jails in Massachusetts do provide recreation facilities; 44 of New York's 74 jails have facilities of this type, as do 35 of Pennsylvania's 73 jails, 6 of New Hampshire's 11, and 71 of California's 134. Hawaii has only 4 local jails, 2 of which have recreation facilities.

Educational facilities are even rarer than recreation facilities; nearly nine in every ten jails are without any kind of educational facility. The most notable exception in this instance is Massachusetts, which has 13 of its 18 local jails providing educational facilities of some kind. About half the jails in New Jersey and New York provide educational facilities.

Medical facilities exist in slightly more than half the nation's jails. The states with the highest proportion of jails providing medical facilities are New York and Maine (86 percent each), New Hampshire (82 percent), New Jersey (81 percent), California (79 percent), Massachusetts (78 percent) and Virginia (74 percent). All five District of Columbia jails and the two urban jails of Alaska reported the presence of medical facilities.

The states with the smallest proportion of jails containing medical facilities are Vermont (20 percent), Hawaii (25 percent), Tennessee (27 percent), Kentucky and Arkansas (27 percent each), Alabama (28 percent), and Mississippi (29 percent). It should be noted that Vermont and Hawaii also had the smallest inmate populations of all the states—twenty-two and ninety-seven, respectively. Tennessee, Kentucky, Arkansas, Alabama, and Mississippi, however, all had sizable numbers of jail inmates—ranging from about 1,200 in Arkansas to about 3,600 in Tennessee.

Visiting facilities in a jail are more likely to be present than the other types of facilities discussed thus far. Three-fourths of the U.S. jails contain visiting facilities. Only five states have fewer than 60 percent of their jails providing facilities for visiting. They are Idaho (43 percent), Nevada (47 percent), Missouri (50 percent), Kentucky (52 percent), and Mississippi (53 percent). There are forty-seven jails throughout the nation which do not have toilet facilities. These institutions are scattered over twenty one states.

Table 8.2 displays differences in the selected facilities by region. On a regional basis, the Northeast has the fewest local jails (226), but the highest proportion of such institutions providing recreational, educational, or medical facilities. Whereas the United States as a whole has 86 percent of its jails lacking in recreational facilities, about 50 percent of the Northeast jails are without these facilities. Educational facilities are to be found in only 11 percent of the U.S. jails, but they are present in 43 percent of the jails of the Northeast region. Medical facilities vary somewhat more by region, again with the Northeast having the lowest proportion of jails totally lacking such facilities. Twenty-three percent of the Northeast jails have no medical facilities, compared with 40 percent in the West, 46 percent in the North Central, and 57 percent in the South.

Table 8.2
Jails without Selected Facilities in Cities with
Over 25,000 Population, and in Counties by Region—March 1970

Region	Number of Jails	Percentage without recreational facilities	Percentage without educational facilities	Percentage without medical facilities
Total, U.S.	3,319	86.4	89.2	49.0
Northeast	226	49.6	57.1	22.6
North Central	1,028	91.3	91.9	46.3
South	1,574	90.5	92.7	57.3
West	491	80.0	87.2	40.3

Across the United States, in county and large urban jails nearly 25,000 cells are being utilized which were built more than fifty years ago. This accounts for more than 25 percent of the 97,891 cells located in these same jails. Nearly 12,000 of these cells are over seventy-five years old, and 5,416 have been in use longer than a century.

On a state-by-state comparison, there are six states where more than 70 percent of the jail cells are not over twenty-five years old. All 57 cells in Alaska's two jails are in this category. About 82 percent of Florida's 2,744 cells are twenty-five years old or younger; 77 percent of California's 7,858 cells are, 76 percent of the 1,219 cells in Maryland, 75 percent of the 3,054 cells in Virginia, and 71 percent of Wisconsin's 1,973 cells were constructed since 1945.

By contrast, there are seven states with more than half their jail cells over fifty years old. In New Hampshire, 88 percent of the cells are older then fifty years. In Massachusetts, Vermont, and Maine, the percentages are 78, 72, and 68, respectively. Sixty-one percent of Pennsylvania's cells exceed fifty years of age, as do 55 percent of the cells in Montana and 52 percent in Kentucky.

Overcrowding

Across the United States, one in twenty of the local jails are holding more inmates than they were designed to hold. Altogether, 205 institutions reported overcrowding, of which 15 percent are exceeding their capacity by 100 persons or more. Fourteen institutions, all located in very large metropolitan areas, reported overcrowding in excess of 300 inmates.

The figures presented on the extent of overcrowding refer only to each institution as a complete entity. Although absolute overcrowding may not occur for a given jail, it is possible for the same jail to be overcrowded in selected quarters. For example, the section of a jail used for adult males may exceed its capacity but the female or juvenile sections may be under-utilized so that, overall, the facility may or may not be overcrowded.

The states with the largest proportion of their jails reporting overcrowded conditions are the District of Columbia (two of its five jails or 40 percent), New Jersey (25 percent), New York (20 percent), and Maryland (17 percent). By contrast, seventeen states reported either no jails or only one jail that exceeds its design capacity.

Table 8.3 shows regional comparisons of overcrowding in local jails. It shows that large jails are more likely to be overcrowded than smaller ones. Considering all jails in the United States, one in twenty is overcrowded. Those jails, however, which are designed to hold between 100 and 299 inmates are twice as likely to exceed capacity. One in ten of these reported overcrowding. For those jails designed to hold 300 or more inmates, nearly three in ten are overcrowded.

By region, the Northeast reported the highest percentage of jails with overcrowding—about 14 percent. The North Central was lowest at less than 4 percent. In the largest jails—300 or more capacity—about four in nine of the Northeast jails are holding more inmates than design capacity permits. In the North Central this ratio is one in three. In the West, it is slightly more than one in four, and in the South one in five.

Table 8.4 shows the extent of overcrowding by the actual design capacity. Thirty-one jails which, by design, can accommodate 100 or more persons were overcrowded in excess of 100 persons on the

Table 8.3—Percent of Jails That Are Overcrowded for Their Design Capacity, by Region—March 1970

Region	Number of Institutions	Number and Percent Overcrowded*	Design capacity					
			1-99 inmates		100-299 inmates		300+ inmates	
			Number of Institutions	Percent Overcrowded*	Number of Institutions	Percent Overcrowded*	Number of Institutions	Percent Overcrowded*
Total, U.S.	4,037	(205) 5.1	3,532	(128) 3.6	374	(39) 10.4	131	(38) 29.0
Northeast	235	(32) 13.6	151	(7) 4.6	54	(12) 22.2	30	(13) 43.3
North Central	1,178	(40) 3.4	1,092	(25) 2.3	71	(10) 14.1	15	(5) 33.3
South	1,914	(92) 4.8	1,686	(69) 4.1	178	(13) 7.3	50	(10) 20.0
West	710	(41) 5.8	603	(27) 4.5	71	(4) 5.6	36	(10) 27.8

*Numbers in parentheses are the number of institutions upon which the percentages are based.

Table 8.4—Number of Jails by Design Capacity by Overcrowding for the U.S.—March 1970

Design Capacity (Number of Inmates)	Number of Institutions	Number at or below Capacity	Institutions Over Capacity By				
			Less Than 10	10–24	25–99	100–299	300 or More
Total..........	4,037	3,832	92	35	47	17	14
Less Than 10	594	572	21	1	—	—	—
10–24.........	1,327	1,273	39	14	1	—	—
25–99.........	1,611	1,559	26	11	15	—	—
100–299.........	374	335	3	8	21	7	—
300 or More	131	93	3	1	10	10	14

survey date. This includes fourteen institutions which were built for 300 or more inmates but which exceed their capacity by a like amount.

Jails by Type of Retention Authority

Of the 4,037 jails in the United States, 3,807 or 94 percent have the authority to hold persons who have not been arraigned or who are being held for other authorities. Of these, 5 are exclusively for females and 2,785 have the authority to hold juveniles under the same conditions. A total of 3,614 (90 percent) of the jails have the authority to hold arraigned persons who are awaiting trial, including 8 institutions that are used exclusively for females and 2,289 that hold juveniles.

Convicted persons awaiting further legal action are held in 2,745 jails—or 68 percent of the total. Nine such institutions hold females and 856 also hold juveniles. Eighty-seven percent (3,531) of all jails have the authority to hold sentenced prisoners for terms of one year or less. Sentenced prisoners serving more than a year are found in only 572, or 14 percent of all jails; 67 of these jails also hold juveniles.

Employment, Expenditures, and Planned Construction

The number of employees in the country's jails in March 1970 was 33,729, including 5,676 part-time employees. Fulltime equivalent personnel amounted to 28,911.[9] Over 30 percent of the fulltime equivalent work force is located in only two states—New York and California—with 4,477 and 4,474 employees, respectively.

The ratio of inmates to fulltime equivalent employees averaged 5.56 for the United States. Variation in this number among states was considerable, however, ranging from high ratios of 11.44 in Mississippi, 10.63 in Idaho, and 10.22 in Texas to low values of 1.31 in Hawaii, 2.70 in Massachusetts, 3.27 in Maine, 3.40 in the District of Columbia, and 3.43 in New Hampshire.

The average earnings of fulltime employees was $617 for the month of March, with the overall March payroll exceeding $18 million. Three-eighths of the March payroll was expended in California and New York, each with over $3.3 million. The average monthly earnings of fulltime employees is almost 50 percent higher in cities over twenty-five thousand population and in counties than in cities under twenty-five thousand—the figures being $620 and $419, respectively. The highest average salaries are paid in the District of Columbia ($849), California ($760), New York ($745), and Wisconsin ($705). The lowest are found in Arkansas ($338), South Dakota ($350), West Virginia ($369), Idaho and South Carolina ($380 each), North Dakota ($392), and Mississippi ($397).

Fiscal year 1969 operating costs amounted to $324 million, of which 42 percent was expended in California, New York, and Pennsylvania. Anticipated construction expenditures for fiscal year 1970 were $171 million, with 48 percent of that total expected to be spent in New York, Washington, California, Illinois, Maryland, and New Jersey.[10]

9

Continuing Topics for Consideration

This chapter is addressed to some of the historic and contemporary issues concerning jails, presented for the reader's consideration and information. These topics may give some indications as to the possible directions jails may take in the future.

Professionalism among Jailers

There is an interest in becoming professional on the part of many jailers, and this has been advanced by such organizations as the National Jailers Association and the National Jail Managers Association. One factor that will probably help in this endeavor is mass communication, which enables jailers from all around the country to communicate with each other. They are able to compare techniques, job conditions, and many other factors affecting their jobs. This may help develop an esprit de corps and lead toward a more professional approach to their job.

Usually there are five elements in "professionalizing" an occupation. First, we find that a professional uses his professional organization as a primary source of ideas and judgment. Second, professionals feel that they are performing a service to the public, one that is indispensable and concomitantly of benefit to themselves. Third, there is a belief that the professional should be self-regulating. Fourth, a professional has a certain sense of calling to his field. Fifth, the professional feels he should have autonomy in his work.

One need only compare this ideal with the current lack of status of jailers in order to see where the field is in relation to that of other groups that are termed professional.

Recruitment and Training of Jailers

Of major concern to some of those associated with jails are the problems of recruitment of jailers and the training of those recruited. In historic times jailers were often recruited from (1) the lower class, (2) the less knowledgeable, or (3) the group that saw the jail as a way of obtaining economic, social, or psychological advantages. Most of the early jailers had little concern for either the inmates or the structures in which they were housed. It took few qualifications to become a keeper of the keys.

Looking into the earlier part of the twentieth century, we find that those who were given the task of jailer were often the new police or sheriffs' officers who were waiting to go into regular police work, biding their time as jailer until a law-enforcement position opened. A second group of individuals assigned to the jail included the law enforcement officers who couldn't make it out on the streets or who were being disciplined for some departmental offense. Add to these a third group, which was comprised of officers who were retired and employed in the jail so as to draw a second income, and you have a good picture of the type of jailers who were running our institutions.

In some locations in the United States, these conditions are still prevalent. In other places, however, the jailer's job is separate from law enforcement, and those working in the jail are required to possess specific qualifications. Many of these are qualified on a separate civil service list reserved exclusively for jailers. In jails staffed by these people, there has been a direct move to recruit individuals who have had some college experience or are at least aware of the disciplines of psychology, sociology, and perhaps even business administration.

Once new staff members are selected, some jails require that they undergo specific training. As indicated in chapter 7, these new employees are given classes in psychology, communications, prisoner treatment, business, sociology, law, and a host of other subjects. It is thought that this training will prepare the jailer in dealing with the many problems that arise in his institution. This is certainly an improvement over times past when the jailer received no preemployment training and very little on-the-job training.

One of the main questions regarding training is who should be responsible for it. Because of their scarce financial resources, many city and county governments are looking to state and federal sources for help.

Architecture of the Jail

Jails in the United States are a heterogeneous group of confinement facilities. Some of them are over 100 years old and represent the philosophy and architecture of times past, while other facilities are newly built. As a result, the designs vary tremendously. If there were more uniformity in design it would be easier to discuss jail conditions applicable to all. As it is, the facilities in one location may be very primitive and in another very advanced, even though geographically very close. Some jails look like modern office buildings, while others appear as medieval fortresses. The interiors of some are safe for captor and captive, while others are a nightmare to work or live in.

Although there are movements by architects to find commonality in design and purpose, there has generally not been a universal set of guides and principles set down by architects or the public. In many cases the local jails are designed by local architects who have little or no appreciation for the special problems inherent in jail design. From a practical point of view, some of those newly constructed present serious design and structural problems for local government and jail administrators. There should be a greater focus on architectural design in its relationship to jails.

Jail Administrators

There has been a movement to identify and train the jail administrators in this country. In many jurisdictions jailers and their staffs have the lowest priority in the law enforcement hierarchy and consequently receive the least amount of available resources. This is slowly changing as there is now evidence that the jail division (when it is under law enforcement) is beginning to interact on a par with other divisions within law enforcement organizations.

One of the areas of concern has been the turnover in the position of jail administrator. Sometimes after a lengthy training period a jail administrator may quit his job because of difficulties he encounters in just trying to keep the operation going. These difficulties may be of a political, social, or economic nature.

In some cases, the administrator may be the sheriff, who appoints a deputy to take charge of the jail. In most instances the sheriff has had little or no concern for the jail either before or after entering office. His main goal is to select an administrator who will run things without causing any trouble. The sheriff may get such an administrator, and this individual may do a pretty good job with the jail, but when the next election occurs the sheriff may be ineligible to run or he may lose the election. The incoming sheriff may want to put his own man in the jail administrator's position. Thus, a jail administrator may work only two or four years and then be replaced by a complete novice. The new administrator may benefit very little from the past administrator's experiences.

It is necessary to recognize these issues regarding jail administration. It is important that a cadre of jail administrators be developed and that their positions be tied to civil service rather than political elections. There is one trend that does seem to be spreading, and that is to move the administration of the jail out from under law enforcement. In these cases the jail is still the property of the city or county but is administered by agencies concerned with correction, rehabilitation, or treatment. In other instances the jail may fall under a department. The administrators for these facilities are often trained administrators who have worked in other bureaucratic organizations prior to their heading a jail.

County-City Jail Model

As we discussed in an earlier chapter, there is a movement on the part of some local governments to merge county and city resources so as to have one jail for both. As a result the jail is located in either the city or county and is administered by either city employees, county employees, or a combination of both. From the perspective of scarce resources this movement makes a great deal of sense. It is far cheaper to operate one facility than two. It is also possible to have a reduction in manpower and to eliminate costly duplications in equipment and other items.

Some of the major problems presented by such a merger include (1) the inability of two local governments to cooperate with each other, (2) the loss of a facility by one of the governments, and (3) the construction of a single large facility, which may be difficult to manage.

With regard to this last point there is a trend in the United States to decentralize prisons and other large confinement facilities. This movement is aimed at putting the responsibility and care of offenders back into the local jurisdiction. Thus we hear people speak of *miniprisons* and their construction. The miniprison concept may in some ways be contrary to the idea of combining county and city confinement institutions.

Regionalization and State-Operated Jails

The dispersal of prison inmates from the large state prisons to the miniprisons is in conflict with the move in some areas toward the regionalization of jails. The regionalization model calls for the closing of many local jails and the construction of a single large jail to confine all inmates in a particular area. This model may further advocate the building of local lockups. These lockups would house inmates temporarily until they either appeared before a local judge or could be transported to the regional facility.

Closely akin to the movement for regionalization of jails is the thrust toward state-operated jails. There are currently three states that operate all the jails located there. Some people have advocated that all jails should be put under the states in which they are located. It is suggested that (1) the states can more efficiently operate the jails, (2) they can see to it that state standards are adhered to, (3) the jails would cost less to operate under the state, and (4) they would not be used as much for political purposes as they now are.

England put her jails under a central form of government in the latter part of the nineteenth century, a move that seems to have met with great success. It appears that those under state supervision in this country are doing well. Because of this there is a group of people in the United States that is recommending state administration of jails.

The Role of the Jail

An important contemporary issue concerning jails is that of their role in modern society. There has probably never been a period in which the jail's role has been so ambiguous. The roles assigned are varied and somewhat dependent upon the location and politics surrounding each particular jail.

First, some see the role of the jail as that of punishment. Those confined are to be punished. Second, others see the role as one of treatment. Those confined to a facility should be rehabilitated so that they will be better citizens. Third, there are some people who see the jail as a source of protection for citizens: the jail protects society from those incarcerated. Fourth, some see the role of the jail as the holding of an individual to make sure justice will be met. This means that a person is held to make sure he will come to trial and that he is held after trial to make sure he receives the sanctions of the court. Fifth, some people see the jail in the role of warning people that if they violate the law they will be locked up. One of these roles may blend into another in actual practice. Some individuals see the role of the jail as a combination of those listed above. The problem however is that there is no clear consensus as to what the role should be.

In most states there is no state direction for jails or their roles. There is no leadership as well from the federal level. It is difficult to assign clear-cut tasks where the role of jail is so ambiguous.

Keeping People Out of Jails

One finds that there is a trend towards keeping people out of jails. Many have recognized that contemporary jails are generally counterproductive to almost everything of a positive nature (they don't even punish well) and may therefore advocate removing as many people as possible from these institutions.

There are many alternatives to confinement. A few of them are:

1. Extensive use of bail rather than incarceration
2. Collection of fines by installment so the person doesn't have to sit his time out in jail
3. Greater use of probation
4. Imposing fines rather than incarceration
5. Decriminalization of victimless crimes

6. Use nonresident treatment programs for certain offenders
7. Diversion programs for alcoholics and others
8. More pretrial release (release on personal recognizance)
9. Issuing summons by police for certain offenses in lieu of booking
10. Using postconviction community-based treatment programs
11. Increasing the flow of cases in the courts so people are held for shorter periods of time

Community Interest in Jails

Jails have always suffered from a lack of public interest. The old adage, Out of sight, out of mind, seems to be particularly applicable. Once in a while something happens in a jail and the public becomes aware of its existence. If a jailer gets killed or a riot occurs in a facility, the news media become interested, which may motivate public officials to conduct an investigation. As a result of the investigation the poor physical conditions of the jail and its inmates may come to light. There may be a temporary outcry, some recommendations, and then the whole matter will probably be dropped.

It would seem that the public should be made continually aware of the existence of the jails, their physical condition, the condition of the inmates, and the conditions under which the jailers must work. If this were the case then groups wishing to initiate change might find it easier. It is our feeling that the jails should be open to public inspection whenever time, security, and manpower permit. They are public facilities that are constructed from tax money, and the public should see what it is or is not getting for its money.

In speaking of getting one's money's worth, it should be noted that these facilities are expensive to erect and maintain. The typical conventional jail with standard hardware costs per square foot about 16 percent more than a courthouse, 40 percent more than a new high school, and 10 percent more than a modern hospital.

Removal of Certain Classes of Inmates

For hundreds of years there have been various movements to take certain people out of the jail population. In the United States there was a movement that began in the early part of the last century to remove juveniles from jails. This movement has only been partially successful, since there are many thousands of children of different ages still in our jails. The children, both male and female, are held for a range of offenses from petty to serious.

There have also been drives to remove the alcoholics and the mentally ill from jails, in which we still find many of these people confined. In the case of the mentally ill, the laws governing the commitment to mental institutions in some areas have become so difficult to contend with that it is hard to confine these people in any place other than the jail. The mentally ill need treatment, and they generally receive very little of it while in jail. Alcoholics are also a group of individuals who need help rather than confinement. Thousands of these people are committed every day and they represent, as do the mentally ill, a medical and social problem.

The jail has been used as a dumping ground for some of society's problems. When other institutions were either not available or full, people were placed in jail because there was no other place to put them.

Safe and Sanitary for Inmates and Jailers

A variety of jails can be found around this country. Some of them are safe for both jailers and inmates, while most are not. Sanitation conditions are probably better than in the past, since there has been a great deal of improvement in this area in the last thirty years.

Many present hazards to the jailers who work in them. Due to poor design and construction, plus overcrowding, there are some facilities in which there are many blind spots where a jailer can be easily hurt or killed by an inmate or group of inmates. In addition, there are problems associated with overcrowding which endanger the jailer as well as the inmate.

There is also a safety factor affecting inmates. In these same facilities that are dangerous to jailers there are conditions conducive to physical and psychological violence among the inmate population. Inmates may intimidate other inmates and exploit them financially or sexually. Thus, the person awaiting trial (and presumed innocent under the law) may be subjected to various forms of brutality by other inmates.

Sanitary conditions vary from area to area, but there are still some jails that are very dirty. Sick and healthy inmates are often thrown together. Physicians may rarely call at the jail, and this neglect may promote the spread of disease from inmate to inmate and from inmate to jailer. There are some jails in which blankets and bedding are rarely washed, and other facilities in which the toilets do not always function or are filthy. In still other jails the processing of the food is not done by the most sanitary methods.

Admittedly, there have been changes over the last 100 years, but bad conditions do still exist. Some of the problems could be eliminated by architectural design and proper construction, while others can be remedied by economic resources and interest as well as care on the part of the jailer.

Research Studies of Treatment

From time to time new treatment programs have been initiated to rehabilitate jail inmates. There is a strong suspicion by many in the field that these programs do little to actually rehabilitate (this view is supported by the high recidivism rates in the populations of prisons). Those insisting on rehabilitation measures dogmatically respond that their programs are working. The nagging question is, Who is right?

The answer to this question is not readily available. We would suggest that what needs to be done is a great deal of research. Only then will we know how effective various treatment programs are. In addition, the research being conducted should be made available so that others in the jail field can have access to it. Unfortunately, it is typical in the United States to have research conducted, reported, and then shelved. We have precious little research on jail programs and very few public forms for its dissemination to practitioners.

General Jail Study and Research

In addition to specific research aimed at jail treatment programs, there should be more studies and research aimed at the jail in general. As in the case of jail treatment research, there has been too little done. There should be more study and research in such areas as classification of inmates, jail design, inmate characteristics, jail construction, management techniques, employment practices, feeding practices, clothing design, jail industries, inmate adjustment, inmate psychology, confinement trends, innovative jails, and educational needs of jailers.

These represent only a few of the possible areas of useful research. Even though confinement facilities have existed for a long time, there is still a lot that needs to be known about the physical facilities, the inmate population, and the jailers themselves. It is important to have a method of sharing the research once it is done. If studies and research are done systematically and widely distributed after they are completed, they should enable us to possess a basic knowledge of the jails, their inmates and their staff. The survey that was conducted in 1970 was a step in this direction.

Public Jail Committees

There have been public committees that have either looked into specific jail problems or served as standing committees operating as a public watchdog. Some of these groups have performed a service while others have not. The question of the value of public jail committees is one that arises from time to time. Too often these committees are viewed by the jailers and their administrative hierarchy as a group of do-gooders who don't really know how a jail should operate. The committees, on the other hand, may see the jailers as a group of people trying to hide their problems by evading public attention. Thus neither trusts the other.

The idea of the public jail committee is probably here to stay. The committees may be beneficial to the jails, especially if they are able to see the poor conditions under which the facilities are operated. These committees can possibly act in support of the jailers and their goals rather than against them. It may also be useful to have them see what is actually going on in jails and thus be a second and more objective party than the jailers when it comes to public reporting. It is important also that such committees exist since it is the local citizens who are paying the bills for the operation of these confinement facilities.

Impact of Court Decisions

Court decisions during the 1960s and 1970s have had a profound effect upon the jails. In many areas they have revolutionized the operation of jails, having had an effect upon inmates, jailers, and administrators. That inmates have rights has been established in many courts. In addition, there have also been cases dealing with the physical conditions of the jails. Court decisions outlining inmate rights and jail conditions have been largely responsible for the change that has occurred.

It is quite likely that court cases on the imprisonment process will continue. And it is likely that the resulting decisions will influence the operation of the jail. The frequency of the decisions of the sixties and seventies has made it advisable and almost necessary to have an attorney available to the jail management. It is too much to expect someone not trained in law to interpret and understand the new decisions or laws that pertain to jails.

Felons in Jails

Although there have always been a certain number of felons confined in jails there appear to be more of them now than before. In the past these violators were housed in the jail before their trials, and upon conviction they usually waited in jail just long enough to be transported to the state prison.

A new situation is presently observed in many jails across the country. Since poor prison conditions have been so publicized, there is a reluctance on the part of judges to sentence individuals to prison; therefore some felons have been sent to jail as an alternative. Some cities and counties cannot by law keep inmates in jails for long periods of time, and consequently judges work around this by having felons serve shorter sentences in jails followed by releases on parole. The problem is that some jails are becoming filled with felons. This is hard on the misdemeanant population, the jailers, and the management. Particularly harmful is the fact that the jails were built to house pretrial individuals and posttrial misdemeanants, not posttrial felons. Posttrial felons are often experienced hard-core criminals who are not only potentially dangerous but also exceedingly disruptive.

Because of this current sentencing practice, an additional function is being added to the jail. The question arises as to whether there has been any compensation to the jails so that they can better handle the new situation. The answer in most cases is probably no, which adds to the problems.

Industries in Jail

Since it is well established that inmates have a tremendous amount of free time, it would seem logical that some type of work be made available to them. The question of industries has been considered in penology for a long time. There is some work in the jails, which often consists of housekeeping tasks used to maintain the facility, but meaningful work is rarely carried out.

Labor unions and court decisions are hampering jail industries. The unions see institutional industries as competing with those in the labor force outside the jail. They realize that items can be built more cheaply inside an institution. They also do not feel that it is proper to pay individuals for working in an institution, especially when law-abiding citizens are hard-pressed to find jobs on the outside.

On the side of jail industries it is important to note that if jails and inmates are organized properly they are capable of producing a great deal of income which can offset many of the expenses of the jail. Industries also keep the inmates busy and out of trouble. These industries may also serve to train individuals in new lines of work which may help in reducing recidivism.

Prisoners may work either outside the facility or within it. Those working outside may be taken to a job during the day and then returned to the facility at night. This constitutes a form of work release which is prevalent in some areas. Those working within the facility may engage in work such as refinishing furniture, constructing furniture, building car engines, operating printing presses, to name a few tasks. One of the problems of working inside a jail is space limitation. Most jails are not constructed so as to house many inmates for great periods of time. New facilities can be constructed and older ones remodeled if there is a push for industries in jails.

Jail Rules

There is no universal set of rules used in all jails. The rules governing the inmates vary from state to state, county to county, and city to city. There are also a number of jails that do not have any rules, thus not providing any directions to inmates.

There should be rules for all jails, and these should be posted so that an inmate can read them. In the event that the inmate is either illiterate or a non-English-speaking person, these rules should be communicated to him. It is also important that there be some uniformity in rules among the various states. This, of course, would be exceedingly difficult. There are variations in the laws in different states and a lot depends upon local conditions and the structure of the jail. But certain basic rules can probably be developed (See Appendix H, Rules for the Guidance of Inmates—County Jail).

Jail Programs

If there develops a belief among those ultimately in charge of the jails that one of the main responsibilities of the jail is to provide treatment programs, then the question that follows is, How extensive should these programs be? Should the jails become involved in full-scale treatment? And if so, should this treatment be of a legal, social, and psychological nature? And if this is the case, where will the funds come from to support such a program?

These are topics that are likely to appear in the future. If jails are to become involved in extensive general treatment, it would seem that this would imply changes in most statewide correction programs involving parole, probation, and prison treatment. It may very well be that the emphasis will shift from prison treatment (which is generally a failure) to jail treatment (which we don't know very much about). If this is the case, we may be talking about a whole different group of facilities that are called jails but may be vastly different from most in existence today.

Volunteers Working in Jails

If we move toward a treatment model and away from a holding model for jails, the question arises as to who will do the work. Many jails are currently using volunteers who work closely with staff. These volunteers help the staff by carrying out many of the assigned functions. Thus, we find volunteers interviewing people for possible job placement, conducting group counseling, running library programs, serving as jail chaplains, conducting educational classes, and participating as arts and crafts instructors. This is only a partial list of volunteer jobs. The point is that a volunteer is free help and if properly utilized may supplement the resources of the jail as a good worker.

Volunteers have offered their services and have worked in jails for hundreds of years, but the use of them is not without problems. Unless carefully chosen, they may present a security risk. Not only might they introduce contraband into the jail, but they could also engage in radical activities, that could upset the operation of the facility. This is an inherent problem with introducing unpaid staff into a jail. Another hitch is unreliability of attendance. A paid employee will show up at work when he is supposed to: if he fails to do so he may either lose his pay or be dismissed. No such sanctions can be levelled against a volunteer, and consequently he may fail to show up at a crucial time.

The advantages and disadvantages of using volunteers should be weighed and considered carefully. They comprise a group of usually well-meaning individuals who will no doubt continue to offer their services.

Maximum-, Medium-, and Minimum-Security Jails

There have been and are jails varying in security. Some of them are clearly of maximum security. This type of facility attempts to make it impossible for an inmate to escape. Here are confined some of the hard-core criminals and those thought to be a threat to the public.

In another type of jail, termed minimum security, inmates are housed on work farms or in regular residential dwellings. Often the only thing that separates these facilities from the public is a three-foot-high fence, and the inmates can walk away if they so desire. These facilities are used for nonserious offenders or those about ready to be released.

The medium-security facility falls between the other two. It is not the escape-proof facility that the maximum-security jail is, and it does not have the lax conditions of the minimum-security facility. It is used for inmates who need security somewhere between the conditions in the other two. Some jails are designed so that they contain all three sections under a single roof.

For a long time jailers have realized that not everyone needs to be held in a position of maximum security; yet most facilities are of this type, which is the most expensive to construct. The problem is to determine who needs which unit. The jailer has some idea of how to sort out his general jail population, but there are many marginal cases difficult to classify. Unfortunately the fields of social science have not supplied any completely reliable instruments to be used for this selection. This is another issue that needs investigation.

Classification Systems

The problem of classification of inmates has existed for centuries, and it still presents difficulties to the concerned jailer. The need for it is clear; the method of achieving it is not. For a variety of reasons none of the attempts at a system has been completely successful. One of the main obstacles has been the problem of space. If inmates are classified on too many variables, the number of cells needed for confinement increases greatly. Probably the best system is to place all inmates in separate cells, thus avoiding all contamination, but most jails do not have the room to engage in this practice. It is clear that it is not a good idea to confine the experienced criminal with the first offender or the material witness. The alcoholic and mentally ill should not be mixed with others.

Jailer's Pay

Of considerable importance is the pay given jailers. At best most jailers receive a marginal living wage. At worst they are unable to live on their income and must supplement it by either working a second job or having their spouses work. The poor pay of jailers has been a continual source of trouble for those employed in this occupation.

As you will remember from your previous reading, some of the early English jails were operated for profit. The inmates were charged for entrance and exit as well as for their food, clothing, and other items. At some points jailers charged large sums to inmates upon their release. If one couldn't pay he was held until he could. Later in America, jailers supplemented their income by keeping some of the state money that was allotted for jail food. None of these sources of revenue is condoned for jailers in America today.

It would seem that the responsibility for jailer's pay must rest with the jurisdiction in which the jail is found, and this means the state, county, or city government. If salaries were raised, the good employees would stay rather than move to better jobs, and in addition, jails would attract a better caliber of employee.

Jailer and Inmate Names

Due to changes in both the language and culture, the names that both inmates and jailers have been called are changing. At the present time it appears that those confined to jails are generally referred to as *inmates.* There is some indication that this may become *residents.* This appears to have the backing of those who believe that there is a stigma attached to the word *inmate.* In the immediate past these people were known as prisoners and before that as convicts, jailbirds, and an assortment of other names.

Jailers on the other hand have been known by various titles. There seems to be a trend toward referring to them now as *custody personnel.* This may be due to the general upgrading in title that many occupations are undergoing. It is hard to find car mechanics but easy to find auto maintenance personnel. A friend recently remarked that jailers in the future may be referred to as custodial engineers! In the past they have been referred to as guards, screws, turnkeys, and a host of rather uncomplimentary names, especially by their charges. At various times there appeared to be consensus as to what the keepers should be called, but at present there is no such uniformity.

This may represent only a temporary problem brought about by rather rapid social changes, but it is still an issue that must be considered. It would help a great deal if there were uniformity in referring to both jailers and inmates.

Code of Ethics

Closely associated with the development of jailers into a cohesive occupational group is the establishment of a code of ethics for them. The two fields most closely allied with jailers are corrections and law enforcement, and both of these occupations have developed their own codes of ethics. There are many norms currently practiced by jailers although not recorded. It is possible that a code of ethics cannot be developed until there is an organization on a national level that speaks for all jailers. It is, however, quite possible to establish such codes within local jails and through existing state organizations.

With the development of a code of ethics comes the responsibility of enforcement. This implies the power to sanction so as to enforce conformity. Who will do this, what they will do, and how it will be done are all matters that must be considered. A code of ethics is a most important issue for jailers.

The topics in this chapter do not represent an exhaustive list. They are presented by the authors for the consideration of those interested in the future course of American jails. The direction that jails will take will most certainly depend upon how these various topics are handled. It is possible that the jail in the next hundred years will undergo much greater change in function and role than it did in the preceding hundred years.

Appendixes

Appendix A
New County Prison, Hartford, Connecticut, 1837

Reprinted from *The 12th Annual Report of the Board of Managers of the Prison Discipline Society* (Boston: 1837; reprint ed.: Montclair, N.J.: Patterson Smith, 1972), pp. 102–4.

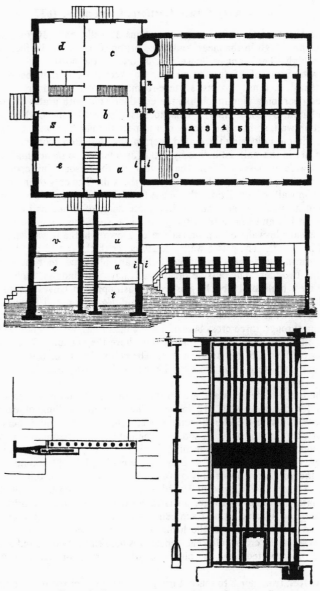

ALFRED SMITH'S DIAGRAM OF THE NEW COUNTY PRISON,
HARTFORD, CONNECTICUT, 1837

New County Prison, Hartford, Connecticut, 1837

The Hartford County new gaol contains 32 cells, each 10 feet long, 5 wide, and 7 high in the clear, and three prison rooms, each 16 feet square, and 8 high. The front or house part is towards the north.

PLAN. Scale of 25 feet to an inch. a, keeper's office; b, bedroom; c, kitchen; d, e, family rooms; s, store-room; i, a close iron door; i, an iron grated door, on a plan much like the cell-doors, but with grates of 1¼ inch round iron, 3 inches apart. This door is placed two inches beyond the partition wall, so that the keeper can inspect the north as well as the west area, without unlocking the grated door; m, is a close iron door; m, is an iron grate, set in the wall, 28 inches by 30; n, an aperture, 6 inches high and 14 inches wide, to pass food from the kitchen into the prison. This opening is a cast iron box, with flanges at each side of the wall. The only openings in the partition wall, which divides the house from the prison, are three, viz., at i, m, and n. Each of them has an iron plate door, so strong and close as to keep out fire and smoke from the prison, in case of the house being burnt.

The outside walls of the prison are of brown Chatham wall stone, laid solid in mortar. The prison walls are 20 inches thick, and 18 feet high, and for warmth and dryness are furred, lathed and plastered, four inches thick, making two feet. The outside prison walls have 10 windows, each 4 panes wide by 8 high, of 10 by 12 glass. The sash opens in halves horizontally. Each window has 7 perpendicular grates, of 1½ inch round wrought iron, drilled 4 inches into stone window caps and sills, and further confined by passing through three cross bars of 4 by ¾ inch iron, the ends laid well into the wall. The height of the window sills above the outside is 7 feet; above the brick paving of the areas, 6 feet. The cell walls are of brick masonry. The east and west areas are each 12 feet wide; north area 6½ feet, south area 3 feet.

The end and centre walls are 16 inches thick, side walls 20 inches, and cross (or division) walls, 12 inches. The floor and ceiling of each cell consists of a single Bolton flagging stone, 4 inches thick, laid 3 inches into the brick walls, all round. A separate ventilator, 4 inches square, opens into the back side of each cell; opening, in the first story, into the cells in two places, viz., one at the floor and one at the ceiling; into the second story of cells the ventilator opens only at the ceiling. Four cells in the first story, (2,3,4,5) have their fronts interlaced with brick work and blocks of granite alternately, and have stronger doors than the rest. The outside prison door is under the window, at o. Each cell has a bedstead of ⅛ inch round iron, 6½ feet long, 2½ wide at the head, and 2 feet at the foot, and turns on hinges set in the cross wall. The bedstead is hooked up by day, and let down at night, supported upon the pine stool which serves for a seat in the day time.

SECTION, from north to south, through the west tier of rooms in the house, and the west area of the prison, showing the elevation of the block of cells and north and south areas, to the ceiling. a, is the keeper's office. t, u, v, are 3 prison rooms, 16 feet square. The inside walls are of 12 inch brick work. The outside walls of u and v, spread, as they rise through the joists, to 26 inches thick; are lined, inside, with brick, well bound into the stone, presenting the four sides of plain brick wall, white-washed, but not lathed or plastered. Overhead is a 2 inch oak planking, well spiked to the underside of the joists, and then lathed and plastered. The only door to the rooms t, u, v, must be approached by going through the keeper's office. t and u, have each one, and v two half windows, containing 12 panes of 9 by 12 glass. The other half of these windows is covered inside by masonry, 16 inches thick, composed of alternate layers of brick and granite, (6 inches thick of each). The grates are of 2¾ and 3 inch round wrought iron, set 4 inches apart, one tier to each window. The window over the outside door to keeper's office, looking upon the stairs, is grated with 2 inch round iron, to keep persons outside from getting access to the stairway. The galleries to the second story of cells are 2½ feet wide, supported upon iron arms laid 2 feet into the wall, of iron 2¼ by 1 inch, and bent to receive the railing, which is 3 feet high.

ELEVATION—PERPENDICULAR SECTION and HORIZONTAL SECTION of a cell door. Scale, ½ inch to a foot. The door is 6 feet high, 2½ wide, and 2 inches thick in the frame and cross-bars. Front and ends of the door-frame is of 2 by ⅝ inch iron; back of frame 2 by ¾. Crossbars 2 by ½ inch. Eleven round grates of 13-16 iron. The round rods are passed through holes drilled in the cross-bars, and have shoulders of 1-16 inch at each end, inside of the frame which they pass through, and are strongly riveted on the outside in countersunk mortices, as are also the tenons of the cross-bars. Lock-plate 6¼ inches wide by ¼ thick, dovetailed at each end into the frame, and fastened to it by countersunk rivets. The lock-plate is flush with two cross-bars, and forms with them a surface of 7¼ inches wide, to receive a lock 6¾ inches wide. The opening at bottom of the door is formed by a frame of 2 by ⅝ inch iron, with two tenons at bottom, and three rods riveted to it at top, and is 6 by 9 inches in the clear. The door turns on a round pivot, 2 inches in diameter, in a cast iron box, which is leaded into the stone door-sill. A like pivot at top passes up into a hole drilled in the door-cap, and through a round hole drilled in an iron bar of 4 inches by ¾, let in flush with the under side of the door cap, and laid 16 inches into the wall. The amount of clear space through this door, for the admission of light, heat and air is 18 inches in width, by five feet two in length. The doors of the cells 2, 3, 4 and 5 have frames 2 inches by 1, the backside; 2 by ¾ front and ends; cross-bars 2 by ⅝; 11 round rods, 1 inch in diameter, and lock-plate ⅜ thick; also iron plate doors, above and below the lock-plate, made to shut close and to open in halves.

FASTENINGS. Locks 10 by 6¾ inches, with bolts 2½ by 1 inch, and 3 tumblers. Also 4 sliding bars of 1¾ inch iron, laid in the wall, and throwing stout studs (at I) upon the upper front corners of the doors. The sliding bars move by levers at the north end of the block of cells, with a strong padlock fastening to each of the four levers. The lock staples are cast iron boxes, opening (only) towards the lock-bolt, 3 inches high by 1¼ wide. The shank and flange of the staple extend 12 inches into the wall.

Appendix B
A Brief History of the District of Columbia Jails

In 1800, when the District of Columbia was established as a city, there was a jail in operation in Georgetown. It is believed that this facility was used by the District around 1805 for detaining those individuals awaiting levy (tax) court trial.

When it became necessary for the then new District government to confine offenders or to detain those who were awaiting action of the court, a large house at New Jersey Avenue and D Street was used for several months. This structure is usually referred to as the first city jail.

The second facility to be used by the District was a small brick structure located on the North side of C Street, a short distance east of 6th Street, N.W. This building is believed to be one of several slave pens in existence in the city in 1800. This particular one may have been used as a jail because it was located near the court.

The third structure to be used was the Circuit Court Jail which was built by an 1801 appropriation of $11,000 by the first Congress. This was a two-story brick building located on Judiciary Square near E Street. The building was ready for occupancy in 1804 and became the only local institution for the confinement of persons convicted of crimes. The building possessed no facilities, not even a yard where the prisoners could exercise.

By 1824, conditions within the jail had become so oppressive that Congress requested the Committee on the District of Columbia to investigate the matter. It was found that the lower story of the building consisted of 16 cells, each 8 feet square. Each cell contained a small window but permitted no ventilation. Frequently, four or five human beings were confined in a space eight feet square for several months with no fresh air. There was no distinction between those serving sentence and those awaiting trial; all were

---

Reprinted from "A Brief History of the District of Columbia Jails," mimeographed (n.p., n.d.).

forced to share the same cells. In 1826, Congress appropriated $4,000 for renovation of the building. This building served as a jail until 1839, when again the overcrowded conditions became unbearable.

By Act of March 3, 1839, Congress made an appropriation of $31,000 to construct a larger more modern jail. The new facility was a three-story brick structure, located at 4th and G Streets, N.W. Because the exterior of the building was covered with imitation stone made of blue plaster, it was known as the "blue jug." The prisoners were transferred to the new building in 1840. It was at this time that the practice of confining insane persons with offenders was discontinued. Public sentiment had made it necessary to find a more humane method of dealing with this problem.

By resolution of the Senate dated February 18, 1862, the Committee on the District of Columbia was instructed to investigate conditions and management of the jail. At that time the institution was under the jurisdiction of the Department of the Interior and supervised by the U.S. Marshal for the District of Columbia. Their findings revealed that the Marshal was unfit to supervise the institution because of mismanagement of funds and brutal and inhumane treatment of the prisoners. He was dismissed and a warden was appointed.

By Act of Congress, March 5, 1872, jurisdiction of the jail was transferred from the Department of the Interior to the Department of Justice. By further act of Congress approved June 1, 1872, authorization was given to replace the "blue jug" with a new structure to be located in the 200 block of 19th Street, S.E.—the present D.C. jail. The initial appropriation was $300,000. An additional appropriation of $140,057.93 was made in March 1875. The prisoners were transferred to the new jail on December 18, 1875.

Appendix C
Police Jails and Village Lockups

I. Importance of Police Jails

The writer was led to propose this study because the city police jail and the village lockup are the most important prisons in our penological system. This statement is contrary to the prevalent ideas of penology, but nevertheless it is absolutely true, for the following reasons:

First, because they outnumber all other prisons, about 3 to 1. We have in the United States about 200 convict prisons, Federal, State, and local; and about 3,000 county jails, making a total of about 3,200. In our present study, the first attempt ever made to ascertain the number of city and village lockups, we have listed 9,260 and estimate about 1,600 more not reported, making a grand total of about 10,860.

Second, because in them the vast majority of law violators get their first prison experience. The offender, upon his first arrest, is frightened, often penitent and open to good influences. The police jails should be so planned and so administered as to use this moment of opportunity. More can be done to redeem the young culprit within 48 hours after his first arrest than in six months after his commitment to a convict prison.

Third, because they receive many times the number of inmates sent to all of the convict prisons put together. The latest report of the United States Census Bureau enumerated a total of 51,936 convicted prisoners committed to State and Federal convict prisons in 1927, which would be about 26,000

A special report to the National Commission on Law Observance and Enforcement by Hasting H. Hart, Chairman on the Advisory Committee on Penal Institutions, Probation and Parole, reprinted from *Report on Penal Institutions, Probation and Parole No. 9* (Washington, D.C.: National Commission on Law Observance and Enforcement, 1931), pp. 327–44.

for six months; but the number reported to us as committed to police jails and lockups in places above 500 population, in six months of 1930, was 1,350,000, which is more than fifty times the number of convicts committed to State and national convict prisons in six months of 1927. Legislatures and State commissions give much attention to convict prisons.

II. Defects of Police Jails and Lockups

Our study reveals that throughout the United States, the majority of the 11,000 police jails and lockups are literally a public nuisance, and are unfit for the purpose for which they are designed.

First, many are located in city halls, village buildings, or fire stations, where they occupy space needed for other purposes, and where dirty, noisy, and drunken prisoners are brought into close proximity with public officers and visitors.

Second, some lockups are in separate buildings, on the city hall square, necessitating architecture conforming to that of the city hall, while others are located on eligible and expensive corner lots requiring too expensive architectural effect which ought to be used to make the building efficient for its intended purpose.

Third, thousands of police jails and lockups are fire traps and not infrequently prisoners have been cremated in them.

Our study shows that of the lockups in the small villages of seven States, out of 393, only 169, or 43 percent, were reported as fireproof. Conditions are better in the larger cities, and we found that out of 1,366 cities of 2,500 to 25,000 inhabitants, 949, or 70 percent, were fireproof, still leaving 323 that were inflammable.

Fourth, many lockups are antiquated buildings unfit for the purpose. In New England, 20 lockups out of 100, taken at random, are more than 50 years old; in Pennsylvania 10 out of 100 are more than 50 years old, and out of 1,366 lockups in different States, 40 percent are more than 20 years old. Practically all of these old lockups are insanitary, without adequate lighting, heating, ventilation, or plumbing.

Fifth, very few lockups make proper provision for the segregation and classification of women, witnesses, and young people. It is common for young and inexperienced prisoners and even children to be thrown into intimate association for days at a time with vicious, depraved, and diseased criminals.

Sixth, many lockups in small cities and villages are used also as lodging places for tramps and vagrants. Our report shows that on the average lockups in places of less than 5,000 inhabitants contain more lodgers than prisoners. This practice works badly both ways. On the one hand, it causes persons who are simply unfortunate to be locked up and treated as prisoners, and, on the other hand, these lodgers who may be dirty and verminous make it almost impossible to keep the lockup clean and sanitary.

Seventh, very few lockups are properly furnished. Usually the prisoners sleep on wooden or iron bunks, generally without mattresses or blankets. If blankets or mattresses are provided, they are seldom kept clean and the bunks are often verminous.

In many lockups one or two clean rooms with proper bedding are provided for women, but generally women of all kinds associate without classification.

Eighth, the "third degree" is practiced extensively throughout the United States, with cruel and illegal treatment and sometimes torture of persons accused of crime, whether innocent or guilty. This unjust practice is excused on the ground that it is necessary "in order to secure the ends of justice."

Ninth, there is a lack of State supervision of lockups. State prisons and reformatories are managed by State authorities and are subject to supervision by the legislature and other governmental agencies. State supervision of jails prevails in many commonwealths.

There is State supervision of police jails and lockups in New York, New Jersey, Minnesota, and Oklahoma. The Pennsylvania Department of Welfare inspects "only on complaint"; Alabama "does not exercise supervision over jails or lockups in cities of less than 10,000"; in Georgia the department of public welfare has "inspected a few village lockups."

New York is the only State which publishes reports of the condition of police jails and lockups. The State Commission of Correction has condemned and put out of business over 60 lockups, yet the last official report (1929) showed 67 lockups that were not fireproof and 57 in which the conditions were severely criticized.

State inspection is absolutely necessary in order to guard against abuses in construction and administration. Abuses in lockups continue because of the general indifference of the local people. State prisons receive attention from governors, legislatures, and commissions. County jails may have State inspection but police jails and lockups generally are left to the caprice and indifference of local officials and citizens of cities and villages where even clergy and social workers pay little or no attention.

III. Scope and Method of the Study

The time and resources available did not permit a complete or elaborate investigation. The study was therefore limited to the following facts: (1) The location of the jail, whether in a separate building or in some other public building. (2) The materials of the building and whether it is fireproof. (3) Provisions for classification of prisoners, juveniles, insane, and lodgers. (4) Population: Reasonable capacity; largest number at one time and estimate of total number received in six months; number present on date of report, males, females, prisoners, and lodgers.

The accompanying questionnaire was prepared, including the above-named points, to be filled out by the officer in charge of public safety building, police station, precinct station, or village lockup, as the case might be. The question immediately arose how to secure replies to the questionnaire, in view of the fact that the committee had no authority to require answers or to compensate the officer. If the questionnaire was received by a police chief or a village constable, he would naturally hesitate as to the duty or propriety of furnishing such information to an irresponsible inquirer, outside of his own community. Public officers are besieged by such inquiries, many of which properly go unanswered.

Figure C.1 is a copy of the questionnaire.

Figure C.1 **Questionnaire Used in Study**

No._____   In case records are not available
Date received_____   kindly give approximate figures.
Description of city police jail ( ) or village lockup ( ) located in
_____ State _____.

(1) Check name under which building containing lockup is known:
City Hall_____   Village Hall_____
Police Station_____   Fire Hall_____
Or is it a separate building?_____
Or, having no lockup, do you use county jail?_____

(2) Check the materials of the building:
Brick_____   Stone_____
Concrete_____   Wood_____
Steel_____   Or_____
Is lockup fireproof?_____
Built about what year?_____

(3) Check any of the following classes which you keep separate:
Males_____   Prisoners:
Females_____   Awaiting trial_____
Juveniles_____   Serving sentence_____
Insane_____   Whites_____
Lodgers_____   Negroes_____
Or_____   Or_____

(4) Capacity and population of lockup: Prisoners   Lodgers

   (a) How many inmates can the lockup
       reasonably hold at one time?   _____   _____

   (b) Largest number of inmates
       present at one time since January
       1, 1930?   _____   _____

   (c) Your estimate of total number of
       inmates received during period of
       January-June, 1930?   _____   _____

   (d) Of this total (c), how many
       prisoners were serving sentence?   _____

(5) Prisoners and lodgers present at midnight, Wednesday, current week,
date _____, 1930:

                               Males   Females

   (a) Number of prisoners over 18 years
       old   _____   _____

   (b) Number of prisoners under 18
       years old   _____   _____

   (c) Number of lodgers   _____   _____

Signed_____

Official Position_____

Kindly return questionnaire to the office of Doctor Hart, Advisory Committee on Penology, 130 East Twenty-second Street, New York, N. Y., in enclosed return envelope; no stamps required.

The difficulty of securing answers to the questionnaire was met by a simple expedient. A letter addressed to the mayor of the city, or the president of the village council, read in part as follows:

> The National Commission on Law Observance and Enforcement, of which Hon. George W. Wickersham is chairman, desires us to obtain information with reference to city police jails and village lockups of the United States, and we ask for your cooperation.
>
> Strange to say, information has never been collected relative to the number, the location, or the condition of police stations and lockups, and we are seeking replies to a few simple questions.
>
> Will you do us the favor to instruct the officer in charge of your police jail or lockup to fill out the blank on the back of this sheet and mail it in the enclosed envelope?

The questionnaires were sent out to about 15,000 cities and villages. The results, except for villages having a population of less than 2,500, were surprisingly complete, as will be seen by Table I, which follows. We are most grateful for the cooperation of at least 15,000 mayors, sheriffs, and police officers.

Every one of the 51 cities having a population above 150,000 reported; this, however, did not mean 51 reports only, but 420, because 38 of these cities have more than one lockup. New York City, for example, returned 45 reports and Philadelphia 43. Most of these 420 reports were made with care and apparent accuracy.

Of the 69 cities having a population of 75,000 to 150,000, 88 percent reported; of the 167 having a population of 25,000 to 75,000, 73 percent reported. Of all the 287 cities having a population above 25,000, 234, or 81 percent reported.

The returns from the cities and villages having a population below 25,000 were much less complete—46 percent of those having 2,500 to 25,000 and 28 percent of those having a population of 500 to 2,500. Many of these smaller places have no police stations, making use of the county jail or the nearest village lockup, while others use the county jail for the detention of police prisoners. Ten tables were prepared as follows:

Table C.1—Condensed statement of number of prisoners detained in police lockups, compared with population of places reporting cities in which they were located.

Table C.2—Complete report of the material in Table I, by States and sections and political divisions.

Table C.3—Prisoners in police lockups, January–June, 1930, in the 51 largest cities in the United States.

Table C.4—Prisoners in police lockups, January–June, 1930, in cities of 75,000 to 150,000.

Table C.5—Prisoners in police lockups, January–June, 1930, in cities of 25,000 to 75,000.

Table C.6—Prisoners in police lockups, January–June, 1930, in cities of 2,500 to 25,000.

Table C.7—Prisoners in police lockups, January–June, 1930, in places of 500 to 2,500.

Table C.8—Showing number of additional lockups reported by sheriffs.

Table C.9—Showing number of fireproof lockups.

Table C.10—Showing number of cities and villages using county jail instead of lockup.

Of the foregoing, only the first three tables are presented in this report, the remainder being omitted for lack of space.

It will be observed from table C.2 that the 234 cities reporting, which had a united population of 43,548,000, reported 1,123,000 commitments to public lockups during the six months ending June, 1930, which is an average of 2,575 for each 100,000 of the population. The most satisfactory statistics are those from the cities having more than 150,000 population, because all of them reported.

Table C.3 shows the number of prisoners detained in police lockups from January to June, 1930, as reported by local officials, arranged by States and population of cities, with a summary by geographical sections.

This table does not include lockups in villages under 500 population, nor does it include prisoners in the cities from which no report was received. We estimate that the number of prisoners unreported would add at least 250,000 to the 1,350,000 already reported, making a probable total for the six months of about 1,600,000, which would be at the rate of 3,200 per year.

Table C.4 covers the 51 cities having above 150,000 inhabitants, showing the number of lockups, the number of prisoners, and the ratio of police officers for each 100,000 of the population. (The figures here given are more recent and complete than those in table C.2.)

The average number of prisoners during the six months ending June, 1930, for each 100,000 inhabitants was 2,173, one-half of the cities being above that ratio. It is surprising to discover that only one other city (Omaha, Nebr.) has as low a ratio as New York City, which shows 758 prisoners for each 100,000 people. New York City showed a total of 52,515 prisoners in six months as compared with 119,589 in Chicago, 50,090 in Los Angeles and 49,732 in St. Louis. On inquiry, Police Commissioner Edward P. Mulrooney explained that the low ratio of lockup prisoners in New York City is due to the fact that a majority of misdemeanants, including about one-half of arrested persons, brought to precinct stations, are served with a summons and released without confinement, whereas in many cities such individuals are listed as lockup prisoners.

In the course of this study we accumulated from the answers to the questionnaires and other official reports a large amount of material showing dangerous fire risks, insanitary conditions, lack of classification, humiliation and degradation of inexperienced criminals, and even of witnesses and insane people not accused of any crime. All of this material is omitted for lack of space.

IV. Remedies for the Defects of Police Jails and Village Lockups

First, provide for at least six classification in every police jail to separate males and females, old and young, sick and well, dangerous and harmless classes. To this end, the system of two or three tiers of cells in a single room should be abolished and each floor should be separate and distinct.

Second, keep each prisoner in a separate cell and abolish the practice of doubling up prisoners or confining 6, 8, or 10 in a single cell. Abolish the practice of allowing prisoners to associate in idleness in the corridors. Usually the confinement of police prisoners is less than 24 hours and very seldom more than 2 or 3 days. In those exceptional cases where prisoners remain for a longer period, they may be allowed to do cleaning or other work around the prison under supervision; but not to loaf and visit with other prisoners. The number of cells should be sufficient to provide separate confinement for the expected maximum number of prisoners in all cases except extraordinary emergencies caused by riots or police raids.

Third, every police jail or lockup should be strictly fireproof. Cells should not be located in inflammable buildings. In the smaller villages where the village hall is not a fireproof building, the lockup should be a separate and detached building, constructed on simple plans similar to the Minnesota plans exhibited in this report.

Fourth, women prisoners in the hands of the police should be kept absolutely separate from male prisoners where communication would be impossible. The best plan is that which is to be followed in the new house of detention in the city of New York, and has been followed for years in Philadelphia and in Cleveland and Akron, Ohio. In these cities women prisoners are kept in separate and distinct buildings of simple construction and without expensive cells and strong locks. In each of these buildings the women prisoners are under the exclusive charge of women. The popular notion that women can not successfully handle unruly and belligerent women prisoners is a mistake. Special telephonic connection with the police department should be available but its use is very seldom necessary.

Fifth, legislation should be adopted to abolish the illegal and unregulated practice of the "third degree" by policemen and detectives. Provision should be made by law, as in European countries, whereby the prisoners after arrest are examined by a civil officer, duly classified and authorized. The police should be required, as in England, to inform the prisoner immediately upon his arrest that any statement which he makes may be used against him. Police Superintendent August Vollmer, of Berkeley, who is recognized as one of the most competent police superintendents in America, has stated that he never used the third-degree methods, but that he obtained more confessions, and more reliable ones, without its use than could be obtained by this unlawful plan. Superintendent French, of Columbus, Ohio, made a similar statement.

Sixth, in every State provision should be made by law for the supervision and inspection of police stations by a responsible State commission, with power to condemn buildings unfit for use, in accordance with the long-standing practice in the States of New York and Minnesota. This legislation should also provide for the inspection of police stations and lockups semiannually by local health officers, on blanks to be prescribed by the State supervising board. These reports should be made both to the State board and to the local authorities. This plan was put into operation in Minnesota in 1895 and produced highly satisfactory results.

Seventh, the personnel of jailers, guards, and matrons in police lockups should be radically improved. They should be selected with care according to their fitness for the job. The place should not be given to a man because he is growing old or has flat feet, or has ceased to be alert. A special course of training for jailers in police stations should be established in the police training schools.

Eighth, police jails and lockups should be intelligently planned by competent architects. In cities they may be built in the top of a police station, with a special elevator, provided the building is absolutely fireproof. In villages it is cheaper and more practical to build a separate fireproof one-story lockup either on the same lot or a lot adjacent to the village building.

We have prepared four model plans for police stations and lockups which are designed to promote the reformation of the lockup system.

Table C.1

Class	Size of places[1]	Number of places	Number of reports received	Percent of number of places	Prisoners detained in police lock-ups: 6 months	Population of places reporting (1930 census)	Ratio of police prisoners to 100,000 population
I	Above 150,000	51	51	100	842,957	31,343,381	2,690
II	75,000 to 150,000	69	61	88	160,506	6,426,300	2,500
III	25,000 to 75,000	167	122	73	119,567	5,778,686	2,069
	Total above 25,000	287	234	81	1,123,030	43,548,367	2,575
IV	2,500 to 25,000	2,500	1,168	46	194,561	[2]10,000,000	1,945
V	500 to 2,500	6,450	1,829	28	32,702	[2]2,000,000	1,635
	Grand Total	9,237	[3]3,231	—	1,350,293	55,548,367	2,429

1. Fourteenth Census of United States, 1920, Vol I, Table No. 51.
2. Estimated population of places reporting.
3. In addition to 3,231 reports received, approximately 1,300 incomplete reports were received from Classes IV and V and about 1,000 from places below 500 population.

Table C.2 Number of prisoners detained in police lockups January–June, 1930, as reported by local officials, arranged by States and size of city

Summary of Police Prisoners

States and Sections	\[Size of city or town\] 150,000 or over — Number of prisoners	Percent of total	75,000 to 150,000 — Number of prisoners	Percent of total	25,000 to 75,000 — Number of prisoners	Percent of total	2,500 to 25,000 — Number of prisoners	Percent of total	500 to 2,500 — Number of prisoners	Percent of total	Grand total (100 percent)
The North											
New England:											
Maine					1,450	58	877	35	188	7	2,515
New Hampshire			2,000	45	587	14	1,781	41	60	1	4,428
Vermont							2,093	99	88		2,181
Massachusetts	39,150	60	10,740	17	8,266	12	6,789	11			64,945
Rhode Island	4,762	60	1,100	14	1,558	20	495	6			7,915
Connecticut	5,317	41	1,931	15	3,632	28	2,046	16	34		12,960
	49,229	52	15,771	17	15,493	16	14,081	15	370		94,944
Middle Atlantic:											
New York	75,283	74	8,911	9	6,225	6	9,756	10	781	1	100,956
New Jersey	12,728	29	13,648	32	9,389	21	7,291	16	1,172	2	44,228
Pennsylvania	101,516	70	15,457	10	11,105	7	16,675	12	1,064	1	145,817
	189,527	65	38,016	13	26,719	9	33,722	12	3,017	1	291,001
East North Central:											
Ohio	73,346	70	2,660	3	11,807	12	14,389	13	1,416	2	103,618
Indiana	9,656	40	7,150	28	4,450	20	3,646	16	180	1	25,082
Illinois	119,589	85	4,229	3	6,377	4	7,687	6	1,954	2	139,836
Michigan	40,125	74	3,397	6	5,434	10	4,103	8	677	2	53,736
Wisconsin	9,953	50			5,034	25	4,743	20	576	5	20,306
	252,669	74	17,436	5	33,102	9	34,568	10	4,803	2	342,578

135

Table C.2 *Continued*
Summary of Police Prisoners

States and Sections	150,000 or over		75,000 to 150,000		25,000 to 75,000		2,500 to 25,000		500 to 2,500		Grand total (100 percent)
	Number of prisoners	Percent of total	Number of prisoners	Percent of total	Number of prisoners	Percent of total	Number of prisoners	Percent of total	Number of prisoners	Percent of total	
West North Central:											
Minnesota	11,836	63	3,100	16			2,906	16	799	5	18,641
Iowa			8,193	57	2,340	15	3,004	21	1,036	7	14,573
Missouri	73,495	98			61		1,180	1	1,044	1	75,780
North Dakota							1,330	87	196	13	1,526
South Dakota					100	8	959	70	311	22	1,370
Nebraska	1,500	35	1,300	31			658	17	735	17	4,193
Kansas			7,200	58	1,220	10	3,455	27	637	5	12,512
	86,831	67	19,793	16	3,721	3	13,492	10	4,758	4	128,595
The South											
South Atlantic:											
Delaware			3,000	88			420	12	65	1	3,485
Maryland	29,814	95			1,131	4	68		333	1	31,346
District of Columbia	24,930	100									24,930
Virginia	5,850	21	8,967	33	5,020	18	5,974	22	1,396	6	27,207
West Virginia					3,600	52	2,216	32	1,068	16	6,884
North Carolina			2,065	12	3,350	19	10,745	62	1,171	7	17,331
South Carolina							2,047	66	1,120	34	3,167
Georgia	10,000	51	3,126	16	2,618	13	2,496	13	1,483	7	19,723
Florida			12,199	60			6,053	30	1,827	10	20,079
	70,594	46	29,357	19	15,719	10	30,019	20	8,463	5	154,152

Table C.2 Continued
Summary of Police Prisoners

States and Sections	Size of city or town										Grand total (100 percent)
	150,000 or over		75,000 to 150,000		25,000 to 75,000		2,500 to 25,000		500 to 2,500		
	Number of prisoners	Percent of total	Number of prisoners	Percent of total	Number of prisoners	Percent of total	Number of prisoners	Percent of total	Number of prisoners	Percent of total	
East South Central:											
Kentucky	6,000	44			2,000	15	5,031	37	618	4	13,649
Tennessee	15,180	51	11,000	37			3,246	10	405	2	29,831
Alabama	6,874	35			7,844	39	4,106	20	986	6	19,810
Mississippi							4,166	87	603	13	4,769
	28,054	41	11,000	16	9,844	15	16,549	24	2,612	4	68,059
West South Central:											
Arkansas			250	6	948	20	2,633	55	888	19	4,719
Louisiana	14,150	76					3,211	17	1,233	7	18,594
Oklahoma	4,405	26	4,500	27			6,422	38	1,394	9	16,721
Texas	35,315	70	4,102	8	5,693	11	5,006	10	902	1	51,018
	53,870	59	8,852	10	6,641	7	17,272	19	4,417	5	91,052

Table C.2 Continued
Summary of Police Prisoners

States and Sections	Size of city or town										Grand total (100 percent)
	150,000 or over		75,000 to 150,000		25,000 to 75,000		2,500 to 25,000		500 to 2,500		
	Number of prisoners	Percent of total	Number of prisoners	Percent of total	Number of prisoners	Percent of total	Number of prisoners	Percent of total	Number of prisoners	Percent of total	
The West											
Mountain:											
Montana							3,506	97	98	3	3,604
Idaho							826	80	243	20	1,069
Wyoming							1,769	95	129	5	1,898
Colorado	10,211	71			1,334	9	2,789	19	206	1	14,540
New Mexico							300	100	14		314
Arizona					3,500	60	2,280	39	135	1	5,915
Utah			5,498	89	190	3	395	6	75	2	6,158
Nevada							2,644	99	68	1	2,712
	10,211	28	5,498	15	5,024	14	14,509	40	968	2	36,210
Pacific:											
Washington	6,850	36	4,281	22	2,509	13	4,807	25	800	4	19,247
Oregon	7,200	81					1,443	17	209	2	8,852
California	87,922	76	10,502	9	795	1	14,099	12	2,285	2	115,603
	101,972	71	14,783	10	3,304	3	20,349	14	3,294	2	143,702

Table C.2 *Continued*
Summary of Police Prisoners

Sections	Size of city or town					Grand total
	150,000 or over	75,000 to 150,000	25,000 to 75,000	2,500 to 25,000	500 to 2,500	
	Number of prisoners	Number of prisoners	Number of prisoners	Number of prisoners	Number of prisoners	
New England	49,229	15,771	15,493	14,081	370	94,944
Middle Atlantic	189,527	38,016	26,719	33,722	3,017	291,001
East North Central	252,669	17,436	33,102	34,568	4,803	342,578
West North Central	86,831	19,793	3,721	13,492	4,758	128,595
The North	578,256	91,016	79,035	95,863	12,948	857,118
South Atlantic	70,594	29,357	15,719	30,019	8,463	154,152
East South Central	28,054	11,000	9,844	16,549	2,612	68,059
West South Central	53,870	8,852	6,641	17,272	4,417	91,052
The South	152,518	49,209	32,204	63,840	15,492	313,263
Mountain	10,211	5,498	5,024	14,509	968	36,210
Pacific	101,972	14,783	3,304	20,349	3,294	143,702
The West	112,183	20,281	8,328	34,858	4,262	179,912
Grand Total, United States	842,957	160,506	119,567	194,561	32,702	1,350,293

Table C.3. Prisoners in police lockups, January–June, 1930.
(51 largest cities having a population above 150,000 [1930 census], arranged by ratios)

Name	Population	Prisoners in police lockups, January–June, 1930		Ratio of police prisoners per 100,000 population
		Lockups	Prisoners	
San Antonio, Tex.........	231,542	1	14,266	6,119
St. Louis, Mo.	821,960	14	49,732	6,038
Kansas City, Mo..........	399,746	9	23,763	5,944
Fort Worth, Tex.	163,447	1	9,043	5,531
Washington, D.C..........	486,859	16	24,930	5,120
San Francisco, Calif.......	634,394	11	32,464	5,117
Nashville, Tenn...........	153,866	3	7,680	4,990
Boston, Mass..............	781,188	21	35,756	4,577
Pittsburgh, Pa.	669,817	16	28,407	4,241
Houston, Tex..............	292,352	4	11,906	4,063
Los Angeles, Calif.	1,238,048	14	50,090	4,046
Dallas, Tex.	260,475	2	10,100	3,877
Baltimore, Md.............	804,874	8	29,814	3,704
Atlanta, Ga.	270,366	1	10,000	3,698
Philadelphia, Pa.	1,950,961	43	71,516	3,666
Denver, Colo..............	287,861	2	10,211	3,547
Chicago, Ill.	3,376,438	39	119,589	3,541
Richmond, Va.............	182,929	3	5,850	3,197
Cincinnati, Ohio...........	451,160	8	14,277	3,164
Akron, Ohio	255,040	1	8,000	3,137
New Orleans, La.	458,762	11	14,150	3,084
Memphis, Tenn...........	253,143	1	7,500	2,963
Cleveland, Ohio	900,429	17	26,139	2,903
Toledo, Ohio..............	290,718	2	8,409	2,893
Columbus, Ohio	290,564	2	7,908	2,721
Indianapolis, Ind..........	364,161	1	9,656	2,651
Birmingham, Ala.	259,678	1	6,874	2,647
Portland, Oreg.............	301,815	1	7,200	2,386
Oklahoma City, Okla.......	185,389	1	4,405	2,377
Buffalo, N.Y.	573,076	18	13,047	2,277
Detroit, Mich.	1,568,662	16	35,394	2,256
Hartford, Conn............	164,072	2	3,517	2,143
Youngstown, Ohio	170,002	1	5,106	2,004
Syracuse, N.Y.............	209,326	6	4,090	1,954
Newark, N.J.	442,337	7	8,628	1,951
Louisville, Ky.	307,745	5	6,000	1,949
Flint, Mich.	156,492	3	3,015	1,927
Oakland, Calif.............	284,063	9	5,368	1,889
Providence, R.I............	252,981	8	4,762	1,882
Seattle, Wash.	365,583	5	6,850	1,873
Dayton, Ohio	200,982	1	3,507	1,745
Worcester, Mass...........	195,311	1	3,394	1,738
Milwaukee, Wis.	578,249	7	9,953	1,721
Rochester, N.Y............	328,132	7	5,631	1,716
St. Paul, Minn.	271,606	7	4,536	1,670
Minneapolis, Minn.	464,356	6	7,300	1,572
Jersey City, N.J.	316,715	7	4,100	1,295
New Haven, Conn.	162,655	1	1,800	1,106
Grand Rapids, Mich.	168,592	3	1,716	1,018
New York, N.Y.	6,930,446	45	52,515	758
Omaha, Nebr.	214,006	1	1,500	701
Total	31,343,381	420	851,364	2,717

Appendix D
Jail Standards of the National Sheriffs' Association

I.   Organizing the Jail
Standards

   1. Only One Jail Administrator. A single officer should be designated as the chief administrative officer.
   2. Jail Objectives. The goals of the jail should be established.
   3. Organizational Structure. The relationship between units of the organization should be diagrammed.
   4. Jail Functions. The principle operational responsibilities should be divided into general groupings.
   5. Establish Posts. Duty posts and work assignments should be designated, defined, and published.
   6. Manual of Procedure. A book setting forth standard procedures and governing regulations should be published.
   7. Institutional Orders. Written directives, providing instructions for new and special situations, should be published.

II.   Personnel Management
Standards

   1. Ranks and Titles. Appropriate designations should be made in accordance with the organizational structure.
   2. Job Satisfaction. Working conditions and compensation should lead to retention of employees due to good morale.
   3. Recruitment. Every potential manpower pool should be approached for qualified applicants.

Reprinted from National Sheriffs' Association, *Manual of Jail Administration* (Washington, D.C.: National Sheriffs' Association, 1970), Appendix C.

4. Basis for Selection. Qualifying and competitive testing should be the means of obtaining employees.

5. Employee Probation. A period of time for the purpose of training, observation, and evaluation should be established.

6. Training. A program designed to prepare employees to perform their duties efficiently and to advance within the program.

IV. Communication
Standards

1. Communication Between Staff. There must be a means of communication between all levels of the jail staff.

2. Communication Between Prisoners and the Jail Administrator. A system of communication between the administrator and the prison population should be established.

3. Communication Between Prisoners and Jail Staff. The prisoners should be encouraged to communicate with all levels of the jail staff.

4. Communication with Counsel. Prisoners must be permitted to communicate with their counsels.

5. Communication with Public Officials. Communication from prisoners to the courts and other public officials must be forwarded.

V. Construction of a Jail
Standards

1. Community Involvement. The support of the community for the guiding principles, construction, and program of the new jail must be obtained.

2. Planning Committee. A representative group should meet frequently to plan the jail. The committee should consist of a citizens advisory group, representation from law enforcement agencies, and the personnel who will administer the jail.

3. Planning Factors. The requirements for construction should be based on the factors affecting the need for the jail such as the projected jail population and the treatment programs to be adopted.

4. Security. The security features of the jail should be suitable for the type of its prisoners and its programs.

VII. Receiving the Prisoner

1. Proper Staff Attitudes. The initial impact of confinement should be mitigated by the attitude and helpfulness of the receiving room staff.

2. Logical Sequence. The receiving procedure should follow a logical sequence.

3. Proper Commitment. Steps should be taken to ascertain that the commitment is legally proper.

4. Contraband Prevention. The receiving operation should include steps to prevent the introduction of contraband into the jail.

5. Vital Statistics. Information concerning the prisoner's vital statistics should be obtained.

6. Receipts. Accurately detailed receipts should be issued to the prisoner for his money and property.

7. Identification. Procedures should be applied to obtain accurate identification of the prisoner.

8. Sanitation. Measures should be taken to prevent the spread of vermin and disease.

9. Physical Examination. Every newly received prisoner should be given a physical examination.

10. Observation and Orientation. The reception process should include a period of time for observation and orientation.

11. Segregation. Determinations should be made prior to the assignment to housing.

12. Records. Necessary records should be initiated.

13. Sentenced Prisoners. For prisoners who will serve their sentence in the jail, a more thorough diagnostic and classification procedure should be applied.

VIII. Discharging the Prisoner
Standards

1. Responsibility. The responsibility for releasing prisoners should be delegated to a supervisory officer.

2. Court Orders. All court orders directing the release of a prisoner should first be verified.

3. Proper Identification. No inmate should be released or transferred until he is positively identified.

4. Processing. No inmate should be released until he goes through the prescribed steps for the type of release.

5. Dates and Times. Days and time of day in which prisoners may be released should be established to meet different situations.

6. Warrants. Prisoners with active warrants or other holds should not be released to the community; but should be surrendered to the proper authority.

7. Readjustment. The jail should take steps to aid in the released prisoner's readjustment to the community.

8. Release of a Dangerous Person. The jail should notify the police of the community to which a released prisoner, who is considered dangerous to society, is expected to go.

9. Deceased Prisoners. A procedure for processing deceased prisoners from the records should be established.

IX. Prisoner's Clothing and Property
Standards
1. Receipt for Property and Money. Receipts should be issued for all property taken from a prisoner.
2. Unacceptable Clothing. Prisoners' property that is considered unfit for further use should be destroyed.
3. Excess Property. The prisoner should be required to arrange for safekeeping of property which is considered excessive and unacceptable by the jail authorities.
4. Handling Prisoners' Property. Prisoners' property should be handled only by trustworthy jail employees.
5. Jail Uniforms. Prisoners should be issued uniforms to wear within the jail.
6. Storage System. A sanitary, orderly, and secure system of storage should be provided for clothing and other property.
7. Transfer or Sale. Transfers or sale of prisoners' property should not be permitted.
8. Prisoners' Money Accounts. The prisoner fund accounts should be kept current at all times.

X. Management of Property
Standards
1. Firearms. Strict controls should be instituted for the receipt, storage, inventory, issue, and maintenance of firearms.
2. Chemical Weapons. A secure and airtight area for storage of chemical weapons should be used.
3. Key Control. The key control system should allow for easy identification and issuance of keys as well as the availability of keys to be used in an emergency.
4. Tool Control. All tools should be safeguarded, marked for identification, and properly accounted for.
5. Control of Restraining Devices. Devices for restraint of prisoners should be available without delay and should be in good working order at all times for use in emergencies and for transfer of prisoners.
6. Dangerous Supplies. Special precautions should be exercised to prevent the dangerous misuse of regular supplies such as cleaning fluids, antifreeze, and yeast.

XI. Special Handling of Special Prisoners
Standards
1. Intoxicated Prisoners. The special precautions to be used in receiving and treating inmates who appear to be intoxicated should be prescribed and practiced.

2. Chronically Ill. The procedures to apply to chronically ill prisoners should be established by the jail administrator and should contain the jail physician's instructions.

3. Drug Addicts. A special program for the reception, treatment, and social rehabilitation of drug addicts should be developed by the jail staff and a committee from the community.

4. Mentally Ill. The jail procedures should include instructions for the segregation, observation, and treatment of inmates who are suspected to be, or have been declared, mentally ill.

5. Sex Deviates. Special instructions should be included in the jail rules concerning the segregation, observation, and treatment of sex deviates, and the prevention of homosexual activities.

XII. Disciplinary Procedures
Standards

1. Communication. As a means of maintaining good discipline, there should be dependable systems of communication among the prisoner, the staff, and the jail administrator.

2. Morale. The environmental condition of the jail should be conducive to a good state of morale; hence to good discipline.

3. Total Effort. Discipline should be the result of the total staff and program effort.

4. Constructive Handling of Violations. Staff training should include constructive methods of preventing and dealing with inmate infractions of the rules.

5. Disciplinary Hearings. A system of positive discipline for treating unacceptable conduct should be prescribed.

6. Limitations on Punishment. Punishment imposed as a result of disciplinary action, must be in accordance with the law, should be reasonable, appropriate to the violation, and based on individual considerations.

7. Records. Any disciplinary action should be a matter of record.

XIII. General Supervision of Prisoners
Standards

1. Sufficient Personnel. The jail should have a sufficient number of personnel to maintain adequate supervision over its prisoners.

2. No Prisoner Bosses. Prisoners should not be supervised by other prisoners.

3. Maximum Observation. Posts and devices should be designed and located to furnish maximum observation of prisoners.

4. Dormitory Posts. More direct personal supervision should be supplied for prisoners in dormitories than those in cells.

5. Schedules. Formal schedules should be in effect for supervisory control of activities and prisoner traffic through the jail.

6. Constructive Supervision. Supervision should be constructive. Every attempt should be made to make it an educational rather than repressive experience.

7. Individualization. Supervision should be exercised with consideration for the individuality of the prisoner.

XIV. Privileges

Standards

1. Communications. Prisoners should be authorized to communicate with relatives and other approved persons and agencies.

2. Visits. A system for conducting visits to prisoners should be prescribed.

3. Commissary. A system for the purchase of items to supplement the jail issue should be established.

4. Program Participation. Prisoners should be authorized to participate in group programmed activities for self-improvement and recreation.

5. Removal of Privileges Not Arbitrary. Removal or suspension of privileges should be exclusively by authority of the Jail Administrator.

XV. Contraband Control

Standards

1. Area Search System. A system should be in effect to provide for the search of all areas within the jail.

2. Unexpected Searches. Personal and area searches must be irregularly timed, unexpected, frequent, and with no exceptions made.

3. Searches with Consideration. All searches should be accomplished with consideration for the individual, but this consideration should not detract from their thoroughness.

4. Supervision. Searches of areas should be made under the supervision of a superior officer.

5. Items Entering the Jail. A system should be in effect to permit only authorized items to come into the institution. All items should also be carefully examined for contraband.

6. Records. Records should be kept for proper timing of shakedown inspections and other uses in control.

7. Prisoners Entering the Jail. All prisoners entering the jail should be thoroughly searched for contraband.

8. Jail Personnel. Jail personnel should be checked for neglect or actions that may lead to contraband getting into the hands of inmates.

XVI.   The Jail Count

Standards

1.   Register of Prisoners.   A register listing the names of all prisoners and their status should be kept current.

2.   The Count System.   A system for taking jail counts should be prescribed and followed.

3.   The Regular Count.   The complete count procedure should be followed at regularly established times.

4.   The Informal Count.   Counts should be taken of prisoners at times and under situations that are not included in the regular count

5.   The Off-Count.   A procedure should be established to be followed when the "head" count does not agree with the count according to the register of prisoners.

XVII.   Emergency Plans

Standards

1.   The Need for Plans.   Plans should be formulated to cope with possible emergencies in the jail.

2.   Comprehensive Planning.   The preparation of emergency plans should be a comprehensive and collaborative project.

3.   Availability of Plans.   Emergency plans should be available to all officially involved agencies and individuals.

4.   Training.   The staff should be trained in the implementation of emergency plans.

5.   Key Posts.   Key posts to be operated during any emergency should be pre-determined and activated when needed.

6.   Plan Activation.   Plans for specific emergencies should include instructions as to who should effectuate them and under what conditions they should be activated.

7.   Prevent Recurrence.   Corrective actions should be taken to prevent a recurrence of the conditions that caused the emergency.

XVIII.   Transportation of Prisoners

Standards

1.   Trained Officers.   Officers assigned to transportation details should be carefully selected and properly trained for escorting duties.

2.   First Steps.   Procedures should be established for planning, preparation, and instruction before the trip begins.

3.   Number of Officers.   A minimum of two officers should be assigned to any transportation detail.

4.   Restraints.   The restraints used should be suitable for each type of prisoner to be transported.

5. Security. Security must be foremost in the mind of the transporting officer and enhanced with proper equipment.

6. Special Requests. As a rule, special requests for visits en route are not granted.

7. Vehicles. Special security and communication equipment should be installed in all vehicles used to transport prisoners.

8. Transportation by Train. Special regulations should be prescribed for transporting prisoners by train.

9. Transportation by Airplane. Conditions under which prisoners will be transported by airplane should be pre-arranged with the airline.

10. In Court. Security measures should be in accordance with the instructions of the court.

XIX. Food Services
Standards

1. Three Meals a Day. All prisoners should be provided three meals a day.

2. Supervision. The food service department should be under the direction of qualified supervisors.

3. Careful Selection of Inmate Help. Inmates assigned to food services must be carefully selected and free of communicable disease.

4. The Dining Area. A dining area should be provided outside the cells.

5. Feeding System. The system of feeding inmates should be included in the rules and regulations.

6. Movement to Dining Area. The rules and regulations should contain a system for movement of prisoners to and from the dining area.

7. Nutritional Needs. The diet should contain all the elements necessary to maintain health and well-being.

8. Menus. Menus should be in accordance with standards established by health and nutrition services.

9. Special Diets. Special diets should be provided when prescribed by the institution physician.

10. No Food Packages. All food consumed by inmates, except for allowed commissary purchases, should be supplied by the institution.

11. Sanitation. The food service department should be maintained in a clean, and orderly, and safe condition.

12. Unusual Situations. Personnel should be trained to handle unusual occurrences.

XX. Health Services
Standards

1. Examination of New Prisoners. Every newly received prisoner should undergo a physical examination before his assignment to a housing area.

2. A Doctor always Accessible. The services of a physician should be available at all times.

3. Sick Call. Sick call should be held daily.

4. Staff. The health services staff should be adequate for the number of prisoners in the jail.

5. Community Health Facilities. Maximum use should be made of community health facilities.

6. Distribution of Medication. The distribution of medications to prisoners should be carefully supervised.

7. Prosthetic Devices. Necessary prosthetic devices should be furnished to needy prisoners.

8. Examining Room. The medical examining room should be adequately equipped.

9. Infirmary. An infirmary should be set aside for the housing of prisoners receiving medical treatment within the jail.

10. Mental Health. A mental health staff should be available for the examination and diagnosis of every prisoner, and treatment of prisoners who are not sufficiently disturbed to be committed as psychotic.

11. Sanitation. A system should be established for keeping the jail in good sanitary condition.

12. Bathing, Washing, Drinking, and Toilet Equipment. Adequate bathing, washing, drinking, and toilet equipment should be furnished to the jail population.

13. Haircutting and Shaving. Haircutting and shaving facilities should be available.

14. Medical Records. Medical records should be kept current for all prisoners.

15. Rehabilitation. Medical treatment should aid in the rehabilitation of prisoners.

XXI. Short-term Treatment Program
Standards

1. Philosophy and Objectives of Short-term Treatment Programs. It is essential that all jails have well-organized, planned, and administered programs for treating both the unsentenced and sentenced prisoners. Such programs may be provided on a full- or part-time basis within or without the jail facility,

but should be varied enough to meet the many different needs of prisoners.

2. Personnel. Staff should be appointed, or utilized, on a full- or part-time basis. Each should be professionally qualified to perform specialized treatment services. A maximum use should be made of the regular jail staff in the treatment process, and of appropriate community volunteers.

3. Physical Facilities. Adequate space and facilities within or outside the jail should be made available to administer proper treatment services, and to separately confine and treat special or unusual and different types of prisoners.

4. The Classification Process. A well-planned and administered procedure for receiving, diagnosing, and treating new prisoners, and for reviewing the status of current prisoners, is mandatory for the proper administration of a jail.

5. Counselling, Guidance, and Therapy. All jails must provide for the diagnosis and treatment of the mentally ill, as well as for regular counselling of prisoners relative to personal or group problems. These services should be supervised by a professionally competent staff, and will involve individual and group programs for the unsentenced and the sentenced prisoner. An institution's staff members should be counselors as well as custodians.

6. Educational Programs. In view of the general educational deficiencies of offenders, intensive and effective programs of basic, adult, vocational, academic, and social education are a most critical part of the total program in the jail.

7. Religious Services. Religion is one of the community's most basic institutions, and thus fulfills an especially important need of those confined in jails. The chaplain provides for worship services, religious education, spiritual counselling to both the prisoner and his family, and is a most necessary person in times of personal tragedies such as death, serious illness, or injury.

8. Recreational Activities and Privileges. To eliminate the dull monotony of jail life, to prevent disciplinary problems, to teach prisoners the constructive use of leisure time, and to maintain the prisoner's family ties, well-supervised and planned recreational activities and privileges are mandatory.

XXII. Community Resources
Standards

1. Philosophy. The maximum use of community resources by the jail staff is essential in preparing the offender for a socially useful and productive life in the community.

2. Planning. The use of community resources should be carefully planned and policies should be established with the community agencies *prior* to their implementation.

3. Staff, Space, and Funds. Where necessary it should be provided *prior* to the active use of the community services.

4. Community Resources. All types of lawful and constructive community resources and services of a public, private, and volunteer nature should be utilized.

XXIII. Community Release Programs
Standards

1. Philosophy and Objectives of Community Release Programs. All institutions for sentenced misdemeanant offenders should establish community release programs for appropriate inmates. It is economical, sensible, and practical to do so. Most importantly, it prepares the offender for a normal, socially acceptable life in the community.

2. Personnel. Adequate personnel on the jail staff should be available to plan, implement, and supervise such programs properly.

3. Public Education and Information. Community release programs should not be started until the private citizens and appropriate public officials have been informed of the programs and their support obtained.

4. Physical Facilities. In any jail system, housing and office space for offenders should be provided, either within or without the institution proper.

5. Work Release. One of the most important community programs that should be established for inmates is that involving employment.

6. Educational and/or Vocational Programs. Wherever possible, appropriately selected offenders should be allowed to attend educational and/or vocational programs in the local community.

7. Additional Release Activities. Other community release activities which will assist the inmate in maintaining family ties as well as socially acceptable relationships with other basic community institutions should be established.

XXIV. Public Relations
Standards

1. Sympathetic Public Understanding. The administration should strive for sympathetic public understanding of the jail, its problems, and its needs.

2. Acceptance. Jail objectives and operations should meet with public acceptance.

3. Informed News Media. The administration should establish a good working relationship with informed and cooperative members of the news media.

4. Effective Recruiting Program. The Public Relations program

should be effective in attracting high-caliber employees for recruitment.

5. Responsibility. The responsibility of the Public Relations program should be that of only one person who operates within the framework of the policies of higher authority.

Appendix E
Course Outline: Abnormal Behavior in the Jail

Washington State Criminal Justice Training Commission
Abnormal Behavior in the Jail. Course 262

This three-day minicourse involves one administrator-instructor and three other instructors. The course is designed so that it can be delivered in different locations in the state.

In addition to the course outline, there is a section outline (Jail Treatment Programs) as well as the objectives of the different sections.

Class Outline

1st Day

8:00 - 8:50	Orientation and Registration
9:00 - 9:50	Pretest and Introduction
10:00 - 10:50	Emotionally Disturbed Inmate
11:00 - 11:50	Emotionally Disturbed Inmate
1:00 - 1:50	Emotionally Disturbed Inmate
2:00 - 2:50	Emotionally Disturbed Inmate
3:00 - 3:50	Jail Treatment Programs
4:00 - 4:50	Jail Treatment Programs
7:00 - 7:50	Emotionally Disturbed Inmate
8:00 - 8:50	Emotionally Disturbed Inmate

Reprinted from course outlines used by the Washington State Criminal Justice Training Commission, Olympia, Washington 98503.

153

2nd Day

8:00 - 8:50	Emotionally Disturbed Inmate
9:00 - 9:50	Emotionally Disturbed Inmate
10:00 - 10:50	Emotionally Disturbed Inmate
11:00 - 11:50	Jail Treatment Programs
1:00 - 1:50	Jail Treatment Programs
2:00 - 2:50	Inmate Characteristics and Problems I
3:00 - 3:50	Inmate Characteristics and Problems I
4:00 - 4:50	Inmate Characteristics and Problems I

3rd Day

8:00 - 8:50	Inmate Characteristics and Problems I
9:00 - 9:50	Inmate Characteristics and Problems II
10:00 - 10:50	Inmate Characteristics and Problems II
11:00 - 11:50	Inmate Characteristics and Problems II
1:00 - 1:30	Inmate Characteristics and Problems II
1:40 - 3:00	Posttest, Evaluations, and Conclusions

Section Outline of
Jail Treatment Programs (4 hours)

1. History of treatment programs
2. Different program environments
   A. Community differences
   B. Jail differences
3. Financing of treatment programs
   A. Local government sources
   B. State and national government sources
   C. Private sources
4. Community sources of help
   A. YMCA, YWCA, Mental Health, Colleges, Volunteer agencies, Social Work Departments (and others)
5. Prisoner classifications
   A. A simple model
   B. Gill model
   C. Other models
6. Classification of Social Services
   A. National Jail Resource Study
7. Types of programs
   A. Pretrial
   B. Sentenced
   C. Released
8. The jail programs (sentenced inmates)
   A. General programs
      1) Religion, recreation, library, newspaper, arts and crafts, trusty

B. Educational programs
   1) GED, college courses, correspondence courses, job orientation
C. Counseling and therapy
   1) Legal, general, family, alcohol, drug, individual therapy, group therapy
D. Other programs
   1) Work release, group living
9. Group exercise
   A. The class will be divided into small groups and given the task of identifying community sources and constructing jail programs.

Objectives

1. To give the student a basic understanding of the role and function of jail programs.
2. To list for the student the types of financial and community help available for jail programs.
3. To present to the student a prisoner and program classification scheme.
4. To list and discuss various programs which may be used in the jail.
5. To give the student an application of the material by including him in small group discussions.

Appendix F
Constitution of the Washington State Jailers Association

Constitution
of the
Washington State Jailers Association

Article I

Name

The name of this organization shall be the Washington State Jailers Association.

Article II

Objectives

1. To standardize throughout the State, insofar as is practical, all procedures, terminology and forms.

2. To promote professionalism of jail personnel.

3. To act as liaison for local jails with the Legislature, Department of Social and Health Services, the Jail Commission, The Criminal Justice Training Commission, and all other organizations which may be concerned with jails.

4. To standardize qualifications and training of jail personnel.

5. To publish information to its members which may be of interest and concern to jails and jailers.

6. To work in cooperation with State and local agencies toward the upgrading and standardization of jail personnel.

SOURCE: The Washington State Jailers Association, mimeographed (n.d.).

Article III

Membership

1.   Except as noted herein, membership in this association may be granted by the executive board, meeting in regular session, upon receipt of application and establishment of qualifications. The membership date shall be that date on which such approval was granted by the executive board and shall become effective upon payment of annual dues by the applicant, where required.

2.   Dues, where applicable, are payable annually on the date of membership. Failure to pay dues within ninety (90) days after the membership date shall cause a member to be removed from the rolls. Thereafter, membership may be reinstated in the same manner as for new members.

3.   Regular membership shall be limited to those who are regularly employed in a county or city jail, as defined by law, and shall not include temporary or part-time employees.

4.   Associate membership shall be open to any person not qualifying for regular membership and may be granted by unanimous approval of the executive board.

5.   Honorary membership may be granted upon the written proposal of any member in good standing, unanimous approval of the executive board and majority approval of the membership at the annual conference. Such membership shall be based upon an outstanding contribution to this association or to the well-being of jails in general. Payment of membership dues shall not be required.

6.   Life membership may be granted to any member in good standing upon the written proposal of any other member in good standing and upon unanimous approval of the executive board and majority approval of the membership at the annual conference. Such membership shall be based upon outstanding service to this association. Payment of dues shall not be required.

7.   The regular and life membership shall make up the voting power. Each such member in good standing shall be entitled to one vote.

8.   Membership of any type may be withdrawn or altered to a different type in the same manner as required for establishing membership.

9.   Retirement from service or change of job status from active jail duty shall not alter the type of membership held prior thereto. However, associate and honorary members who become full-time jail employees are then qualified for regular membership.

Article IV

Executive Board

1.   Members of the executive board shall be elected from those regular and life members who are in good standing. Failure to remain in good standing shall cause such member to be removed from elective office.

2. The executive board shall consist of eleven members and shall include all officers and representatives duly elected by the body or otherwise appointed as herein provided, plus the immediate past president.

3. Officers shall consist of a president, first vice president, second vice president, third vice president, secretary-treasurer and editor. Due to the volume of work involved consideration shall be given to electing retired members to the offices of secretary-treasurer and editor.

4. Officers to be elected at each annual conference are the third vice president, secretary-treasurer and editor.

5. The position of president shall be filled each year at the annual conference by the former first vice president, and the second and third vice presidents shall ascend one step in position. Terms of office shall begin and end at the close of the final session of the annual conference.

6. In the event of a vacancy during the year in the position of president, the vice presidents shall each ascend one step, with the first vice president assuming the position of president.

7. In the event of a vacancy during the year in any of the vice presidential positions, a fifth representative shall be appointed to restore the total number of members to eleven (11). At the next annual conference another vice president shall be elected, in addition to that one which shall be elected annually, to fill the vacated position.

8. Of the four representatives two shall be elected to one-year terms at the first annual conference and two shall be elected to two-year terms at that time. Thereafter two representatives shall be elected to two-year terms at each annual conference.

9. Due to the population ratio within the State, six members shall be from jurisdictions west of the Cascade Mountains and five shall be from the east thereof.

10. Of the eleven executive board members at least two shall be elected to one shall be elected to represent each of the following categories: 1) supervisory custody personnel, 2) female custody personnel, 3) managers of small jails, 4) administrators of larger jails, 5) treatment personnel and 6) retirees. When each of the above categories has been filled as stated, the categories may be disregarded in electing the remaining officers and representatives. Should there be a change of job status by any one individual on the executive board during his tenure in office, resulting in the loss of representation for one category, no action need be taken until a vacancy occurs or until the next annual election, whichever shall occur first.

11. The executive board shall have charge of all interests of this association and shall have authority to act in official capacity on behalf of the membership, except as otherwise stated herein. It shall consider and report all proposed measures for the benefit of the membership and the general

welfare of the association. It shall adopt ways and means for the purpose of advancement of the association.

12. All vacancies occurring on the executive board shall be filled by presidential appointment upon recommendation and/or concurrence of its existing members.

13. The executive board shall direct all expenditures from funds of the association but shall have no authority to financially encumber the membership beyond the extent of those funds.

14. The annual membership dues shall be established by the executive board in an amount not substantially greater than may reasonably be anticipated to keep the treasury solvent while pursuing the goals of the association.

15. Seven of the members of the executive board shall constitute a quorum for purposes of conducting association business.

16. The executive board shall meet at least four times each year at a time and place designated by the president, to conduct the official business of this association.

17. The president is empowered to call a special meeting of the executive board if, in his opinion, such meeting is justified. A special meeting of the executive board may also be called by any voting member in good standing upon consent of a majority of the board members.

18. A sergeant-at-arms may be appointed by the president on either a temporary or annual basis, to serve at any or all meetings of the association.

Article V

Duties of the Officers

1. The duties of the president are to:
   A. preside at all meetings of both the membership and the executive board;
   B. appoint committees as provided herein;
   C. cast the deciding vote in the event of a tie vote;
   D. provide direction and inspiration for members by assuming a leadership role;
   E. upon termination of office, turn over all of the president's records to his successor; and
   F. at the end of his term, take up the position of past president on the executive board, unless elected to another office.

2. The duties of the first vice president are to:
   A. serve as a member of the executive board, and
   B. perform the duties of the president in the absence of the latter.

3. The duties of the second vice president are to:
   A. serve as a member of the executive board, and

B. perform the duties of the president in the absence of both the president and the first vice president.

4. The duties of the third vice president are to:
   A. serve as a member of the executive board; and
   B. perform the duties of the president in the absence of the president, the first vice president and the second vice president.

5. The duties of the secretary-treasurer are to:
   A. serve as a member of the executive board;
   B. record the minutes of all official meetings of the executive board and the membership, and to retain the original set of such minutes in a permanent file;
   C. maintain the necessary correspondence, retaining copies thereof in a permanent file and providing similar copies to the president;
   D. notify in writing all appropriate members of regular and special meetings;
   E. maintain the membership records in such manner that current and complete data on each member is available at all times;
   F. maintain the financial records, including an accurate and up-to-date ledger of all income and expenditures, plus supporting documentation for each transaction;
   G. provide a written financial report at each regular meeting of the membership and executive board, and at any other reasonable time upon request of any voting member in good standing;
   H. notify members in writing of their membership dues approximately thirty (30) days prior to their due date;
   I. collect all incoming funds and pay all approved expenditures of the association;
   J. issue membership cards and certificates to eligible members;
   K. deposit association funds in a bank of his choice, upon notification of the executive board and issue checks thereon for approved expenditures, which checks shall be signed by both the president and the secretary-treasurer; except that upon approval of the executive board the president may waive the signing of such checks;
   L. release all records, correspondence, equipment, monies and other property of the association to his successor within ten (10) days of the termination of his office;
   M. obtain a fidelity bond at the expense of the association, to assure the funds, equipment and supplies under his control, in an amount to be determined by the executive board.

6. The duties of the editor are to:
   A. collect and disseminate information to and from the membership, including the surveying of current legislation relating to jails, and activities of the State Jail Commission;

B. prepare, have printed and distribute association publications at a time interval to be determined by the executive board;

C. act as information officer to the National Jail Managers Association, the Washington State Law Enforcement Association, the Washington Association of Sheriffs and Police Chiefs, the Washington Corrections Association and all other organizations to which this association may reasonably relate.

7. The duties of the sergeant-at-arms are to:

A. assist the presiding officer in preserving order at meetings;

B. assist with the general arrangement of meetings;

C. receive and welcome guests at meetings, acting as a receptionist and presenting guests to the presiding officer;

D. preside over elections by enforcing the election rules and to supervise the counting and reporting of ballots.

Article VI

Committees

1. Committee chairmen shall be appointed by the president, who may also appoint other committee members or defer such appointments to the respective committee chairmen.

2. All committee appointees shall be voting members in good standing. Failure to remain in good standing shall preclude any member from continued committee participation.

3. Committees and subcommittees may be appointed for any appropriate purpose and shall include the following:

A. Constitution and By-Laws

B. Membership and Awards

C. Legislative

D. Training

E. Nominating

F. Program

4. Duties of the Constitution and By-Laws committee shall be to:

A. Review the Constitution and by-laws for clarity of intent, including omissions, duplications and contradictions;

B. Receive proposals for amendments from the membership;

C. Draft all proposed amendments in constitutional form and present them to the membership at the next general business meeting, together with recommendations for approval or disapproval; and

D. Monitor the proceedings of the association for constitutionality.

5. Duties of the Membership and Awards committee shall be to:

A. Actively recruit new members;

B. Encourage lapsed members to renew their membership; and

C. Recommend to the executive board recipients for such awards as may be approved by the membership.

6. Duties of the Legislative committee shall be to:

A. Act as a liaison with the Legislature and with individuals having authority over matters of legislative interest to the association;

B. Draft specific proposals in legislative matters as determined by the executive board; and

C. Propose to the executive board action in matters of legislative concern to the association.

7. Duties of the Training committee shall be to:

A. Monitor jailer training needs;

B. Propose appropriate action to meet such needs; and

C. Act as a liaison with agencies and persons providing jailer training.

8. The duties of the Nominating committee shall be to conduct annual elections in the manner outlined in ARTICLE VIII, paragraphs 3 and 4, under the supervision of the Sergeant-At-Arms, as outlined in ARTICLE V, paragraph 7, item D.

9. The duties of the Program Committee shall be to:

A. Recommend to the executive board probable site(s) for the annual conference;

B. Do complete planning and make complete arrangements for the annual conference;

C. Prepare, have published and circulate to the membership, conference programs and other pertinent material, in cooperation with the secretary-treasurer and the editor; and

D. Conduct the annual conference under the supervision of the president.

Article VII

The Annual Conference

1. The annual conference shall be held at a time and place designated by the executive board after considering recommendations by the program committee.

2. All general business matters of this association shall be determined by majority vote of those eligible voters who are present and voting at the annual business meeting.

3. The agenda of the annual business meeting shall be:

A. Call to order

B. Reading of the minutes of the last annual business meeting

C. Presentation of the financial report for the period since the last annual business meeting

    D. Correspondence of general interest and concern
    E. Committee reports
    F. Unfinished business
    G. New business
    H. Election of officers and representatives
    I. Adjournment

4. During the annual conference the president may appoint a committee of three eligible voting members, assisted by the secretary-treasurer, to review the financial records. Said committee shall submit to the president a written report of its findings, which shall be read at the annual business meeting and retained in the permanent records. Said committee shall include in its report the following determinations:

    A. That the ledger balance is equal to the sum of 1) the checkbook balance, plus 2) the savings account balance, plus 3) any investments balance, plus 4) any checks or cash not yet deposited, plus 5) any authorized cash fund balance.

    B That documentation exists for all transactions, including the following:
        a. checking deposit receipts
        b. savings deposit receipts
        c. investments receipts
        d. purchase receipts
        e. dues receipts
        f. cancelled checks
        g. bank, savings and investments statements

5. As an alternative to the committee action described in paragraph 4, above, the executive board may elect to have the same procedure conducted by a competent, professional accountant of its own choosing within thirty (30) days prior to the annual meeting.

6. Any discrepancies, errors or omissions in the financial records, as determined by either the review committee or the accountant, shall be referred to the membership, which may dispose of the matter at the annual business meeting or refer it for further study to the review committee or to the executive board.

Article VIII

Elections

1. Elections shall be determined by a majority of those voting members who are present and voting at a meeting of the association.

2. All officers shall be elected for one year or until their successors are elected, except as stipulated herein for vice presidents.

3. Prior to the annual election the secretary-treasurer shall provide the nominating committee with a list of candidates who are qualified for each

vacancy to be filled, together with a listing of their qualifications. Such list shall be compiled without favoritism to any member or group of members, except as specified herein. Upon receipt of said list the nominating committee shall make its selections therefrom.

4. The nominating committee shall submit a list of two or more nominees for each position to be filled. Upon presentation of such list to the membership the nominating committee chairman shall announce that nominations are also open from the floor, together with the qualifications for each position to be filled. All candidates thus duly nominated, whether by the nominating committee or from the floor, shall receive equal treatment during the election.

Article IX

Amendments to The Constitution

1. A two-thirds majority of those eligible members present and voting at a general business meeting of the association shall be required to amend the constitution.

2. The Consitution and By-Laws committee shall review all proposed amendments for clarity and for duplication or contradiction with existing wording before such proposal is considered by the membership for passage.

3. By-Laws may be adopted by the executive board for purposes of clarifying or implementing the constitution, provided that no by-law shall be in contradiction of or go beyond the scope and general intent of the constitution.

4. At each general business meeting of the association the Constitution and By-Laws committee shall submit those by-laws adopted by the executive board during the previous year as proposed amendments to the constitution, except as herein specified.

5. The amount of the annual dues shall be specified in the By-Laws.

Article X

Removal of Elected Officials

Any officer or representative may be removed from position for malfeasance or misfeasance of office or for failure to attend three board meetings without excused absence in any year. Such action shall be taken upon an affirmative vote of at least two-thirds of the executive board. Any voting member of the body who is in good standing may bring charges against an officer or representative in a meeting of the executive board, which shall then conduct a hearing into the charges and may hear testimony for and against the accused. Since the executive board is without authority to impose legal sanctions, legal counsel shall not be heard, although the accused shall have the right to have one other voting member in good standing consult with him/her during the hearing. The decision of the executive board shall be final, except that by majority vote it may reconsider the case at a later date upon receipt of new information.

Article XI

Rules of Order

1. When any question comes before this association for which no provisions have been made in the constitution and by-laws, the presiding officer shall be governed by the rules as set forth in Robert's Rules of Order.

2. Except for executive sessions, all meetings of the association, including those of its executive board and committees, shall be open to all members and each member shall have the right of discussion on any question.

3. The executive board, by majority vote of its members present and voting, shall have the right to hold executive sessions to hear matters which might otherwise tend to embarrass, demean or incriminate persons. No official action shall be taken in such executive session without knowledge of the membership.

4. On all questions coming before the membership voting may be taken verbally or by count of hands; except that elections shall be conducted by secret ballot.

Article XII

Ethics

1. This association shall at no time endorse, recommend or otherwise contribute to any candidate for political office.

2. No member of this association shall use the association or his/her membership in it to further any personal or political aspirations; nor shall the association as a body take part in any movement not in keeping with its objectives as stated in ARTICLE II.

Appendix G
Tables from National Jail Census, 1970

Reprinted from *National Jail Census, 1970* (Washington, D.C.: Law Enforcement Assistance Administration, U.S. Department of Justice, 1971), pp. 9-18.

Table G.1 Number of Jails, Employees, Inmate Population and Current Operating and Planned Construction Expenditures, for the U.S. and by State

State	Number of Jails	Number of Jail Employees (full-time equivalent)	Inmate Population March 15, 1970	Ratio of Inmates to Full-time equivalent employees	Operating Costs Fiscal Year 1969 ($000)	Planned Construction Expenditures Fiscal Year 1970 ($000)
U.S. total	4,037	28,911	160,863	5.56	324,278	170,849
Cities with population of 25,000 or more, and counties	3,319	28,435	156,816	5.51	318,431	167,412
Cities with population under 25,000	718	476	4,047	8.50	5,787	3,437
Alabama	107	320	3,018	9.43	3,184	2,218
Alaska	8	40	171	4.28	477	1
Arizona	39	241	2,142	7.23	2,465	692
Arkansas	110	129	1,224	9.49	1,371	141
California	166	4,474	27,672	6.19	60,825	13,982
Colorado	78	311	1,481	4.76	2,894	1,642
Connecticut[1]	—	—	—	—	—	—
Delaware[1]	—	—	—	—	—	—
District of Columbia	5	948	3,222	3.40	14,790	1,686
Florida	167	1,393	9,412	6.76	13,781	2,850
Georgia	240	1,109	6,726	6.06	10,249	2,158
Hawaii	4	74	97	1.31	614	—
Idaho	61	41	436	10.63	468	172
Illinois	108	1,262	5,324	4.22	10,382	13,384
Indiana	97	470	2,685	5.71	4,850	7,262
Iowa	93	110	691	6.28	1,150	153
Kansas	123	133	1,100	8.27	1,449	1,222
Kentucky	148	319	2,693	8.44	2,880	3,795
Louisiana	95	522	4,039	7.74	4,417	4,500
Maine	16	74	242	3.27	624	1,277
Maryland	23	514	2,758	5.37	5,154	11,944
Massachusetts	18	788	2,126	2.70	9,221	9,074
Michigan	92	996	5,789	5.81	12,378	9,985

State	Number of Jails	Number of Jail Employees (full-time equivalent)	Inmate Population March 15, 1970	Ratio of Inmates to Full-time equivalent employees	Operating Costs Fiscal Year 1969 ($000)	Planned Construction Expenditures Fiscal Year 1970 ($000)
Minnesota	77	308	1,476	4.79	3,632	3,042
Mississippi	98	143	1,636	11.44	1,578	543
Missouri	144	489	2,958	6.05	4,598	1,109
Montana	68	51	367	7.20	554	1,134
Nebraska	99	87	823	9.46	769	339
Nevada	23	111	755	6.80	1,036	1,620
New Hampshire	11	97	333	3.43	703	42
New Jersey	32	1,210	4,436	3.67	12,308	10,569
New Mexico	44	128	961	7.51	1,147	2,067
New York	75	4,477	17,399	3.89	57,142	18,041
North Carolina	100	330	2,580	7.82	2,795	3,205
North Dakota	50	22	158	7.18	271	198
Ohio	160	1,093	5,920	5.42	11,826	7,433
Oklahoma	112	226	2,214	9.80	2,554	1,848
Oregon	69	245	1,487	6.07	3,279	1,567
Pennsylvania	77	1,774	6,900	3.89	19,467	7,419
Rhode Island[1]	—	—	—	—	—	—
South Carolina	111	591	3,281	5.55	4,413	459
South Dakota	60	32	307	9.59	395	83
Tennessee	116	547	3,622	6.62	4,912	142
Texas	325	1,049	10,720	10.22	10,848	973
Utah	34	74	522	7.05	729	313
Vermont	6	—	22	—	19	—
Virginia	96	636	3,416	5.37	4,723	3,542
Washington	83	348	2,277	6.54	4,218	14,210
West Virginia	61	140	1,094	7.81	1,290	206
Wisconsin	75	404	1,978	4.90	4,713	2,182
Wyoming	33	33	173	5.24	276	425

[1]Jails are not locally administered but rather are operated by the State government.

Table G.2 Inmate Population of Jails by Type of Retention, by Sex and Age (Adult or Juvenile), for the U.S. and by State—March 1970

State	Total inmate population				Type of Retention							
					Persons held for other authorities or not yet arraigned				Persons arraigned and awaiting trial			
	Total	Adult Male	Adult Female	Juvenile	Total	Adult Male	Adult Female	Juvenile	Total	Adult Male	Adult Female	Juvenile
U.S. total	160,863	145,324	7,739	7,800	27,460	23,552	1,804	2,104	55,619	50,145	2,420	3,054
Cities with population of 25,000 or more, and counties	156,816	141,590	7,539	7,687	25,767	22,036	1,721	2,010	54,997	49,575	2,380	2,042
Cities with population under 25,000	4,047	3,734	200	113	1,693	1,516	83	94	622	570	40	12
Alabama	3,018	2,793	138	87	783	668	50	65	814	763	31	20
Alaska	171	136	33	2	46	39	6	1	9	6	3	7
Arizona	2,142	2,005	104	33	223	191	13	19	664	636	21	7
Arkansas	1,224	1,136	43	45	373	318	20	35	334	318	12	4
California	27,672	25,759	1,725	188	3,428	2,909	386	143	9,292	8,692	560	40
Colorado	1,481	1,356	78	47	341	282	26	33	639	594	35	10
Connecticut[1]	—	—	—	—	—	—	—	—	—	—	—	—
Delaware[1]	—	—	—	—	—	—	—	—	—	—	—	—
District of Columbia	3,222	3,158	62	2	10	8	—	2	923	893	30	—
Florida	9,412	8,719	551	142	2,054	1,831	119	104	2,680	2,526	131	23
Georgia	6,726	6,367	227	132	1,272	1,090	70	112	1,480	1,394	67	19
Hawaii	97	95	2	—	30	30	—	—	31	31	—	—
Idaho	436	380	14	42	128	101	4	23	109	95	5	9
Illinois	5,324	4,980	238	106	1,979	1,811	111	57	1,529	1,434	62	33
Indiana	2,685	2,328	108	249	751	564	48	139	1,049	939	30	80
Iowa	691	629	21	41	180	151	6	23	189	166	8	15
Kansas	1,100	981	44	75	238	189	10	39	421	388	14	19
Kentucky	2,693	2,532	83	78	653	576	25	52	874	838	21	15
Louisiana	4,039	3,813	165	61	940	843	41	56	1,332	1,273	56	3
Maine	242	236	4	2	52	50	1	1	30	30	—	—
Maryland	2,758	2,532	120	106	246	192	23	31	1,730	1,596	64	70
Massachusetts	2,126	2,081	45	—	6	6	—	—	668	632	36	—
Michigan	5,789	5,329	431	29	385	364	8	13	2,331	2,205	116	10

Table G.2—Continued

State	Total inmate population				Type of Retention											
					Persons held for other authorities or not yet arraigned					Persons arraigned and awaiting trial					
		Adult				Adult				Adult		
	Total	Male	Female	Juvenile	Total	Male	Female	Juvenile	Total	Male	Female	Juvenile
Minnesota	1,476	1,358	45	73	236	182	15	39	251	242	4	5
Mississippi	1,636	1,496	66	74	405	341	24	40	460	444	12	4
Missouri	2,958	2,768	135	55	409	347	24	38	1,246	1,182	49	15
Montana	367	302	12	53	140	87	3	50	60	56	3	1
Nebraska	823	745	34	44	164	123	12	29	163	148	10	5
Nevada	755	682	58	15	270	250	12	8	202	174	26	2
New Hampshire	333	327	6	—	48	44	4	—	59	59	—	—
New Jersey	4,436	4,135	175	126	881	801	22	58	1,723	1,608	68	47
New Mexico	961	876	39	46	281	235	12	34	198	187	6	5
New York	17,399	11,970	879	4,550	1,415	965	271	179	7,292	4,993	142	2,157
North Carolina	2,580	2,419	124	37	713	651	35	27	1,170	1,107	55	8
North Dakota	158	149	6	3	56	54	—	2	38	37	—	1
Ohio	5,920	5,423	294	203	1,416	1,222	60	134	1,646	1,537	76	33
Oklahoma	2,214	2,071	95	48	437	375	32	30	738	682	44	12
Oregon	1,487	1,372	56	59	242	172	16	54	467	448	14	5
Pennsylvania	6,900	6,404	242	254	1,223	1,135	37	51	2,915	2,584	140	191
Rhode Island[1]	3,281	3,166	74	41	389	343	16	30	642	614	18	10
South Carolina	307	270	11	26	90	71	3	16	85	78	1	6
South Dakota	3,622	3,419	124	79	591	535	31	25	1,182	1,107	39	36
Tennessee	10,720	10,034	517	169	2,335	2,115	89	131	5,319	5,018	266	35
Texas	522	485	27	10	120	102	9	9	206	194	12	—
Utah	22	22	—	—	4	4	—	—	16	16	—	—
Vermont	3,416	3,028	216	172	516	415	49	52	1,024	920	52	52
Virginia	2,277	2,079	158	40	492	419	37	36	621	584	33	4
Washington	1,094	1,001	41	52	246	204	12	30	284	250	15	19
West Virginia	1,978	1,833	66	79	171	117	9	45	447	394	33	20
Wisconsin	173	145	3	25	42	30	3	9	37	33	—	4

[1]Jails are not locally administered but rather are operated by the State government.

171

Table G.3 Number of Jails by Type of Retention Authority, by Sex and Age (Adult or Juvenile), for the U. S. and by State

State	Total number of institutions	Type of Retention Authority							
		Number holding persons not yet arraigned or being held for other authorities				Number holding persons arraigned and awaiting trial			
		Adult			Juvenile	Adult			Juvenile
		Male only	Female only	Male & female		Male only	Female only	Male & female	
U. S. total	4,037	477	5	3,325	2,785	477	8	3,129	2,289
Cities with population of 25,000 or more, and counties	3,319	324	5	2,765	2,411	343	8	2,695	2,094
Cities with population under 25,000	718	153	—	560	374	134	—	434	195
Alabama	107	6	—	101	82	6	—	95	69
Alaska	8	1	—	6	4	1	—	6	2
Arizona	39	10	—	29	21	9	—	79	17
Arkansas	110	17	—	93	77	19	—	84	62
California	166	29	2	95	77	27	2	67	35
Colorado	78	18	—	57	55	14	—	56	51
Connecticut[1]	—	—	—	—	—	—	—	—	—
Delaware[1]	—	—	—	—	—	—	—	—	—
District of Columbia	5	—	—	—	—	—	1	1	1
Florida	167	23	—	127	75	28	—	114	57
Georgia	240	36	—	160	109	39	—	150	76
Hawaii	4	—	—	4	2	—	—	4	1
Idaho	61	14	—	47	50	13	—	44	42
Illinois	108	20	—	88	86	19	—	82	75
Indiana	97	15	—	82	85	17	—	79	79
Iowa	93	12	—	81	78	12	1	77	65
Kansas	123	23	—	99	95	21	—	98	83
Kentucky	148	24	—	123	103	23	—	120	90
Louisiana	95	11	—	81	68	10	—	81	47
Maine	16	—	—	15	15	—	—	14	13
Maryland	23	2	—	21	19	2	—	21	18
Massachusetts	18	1	—	14	6	1	—	14	7
Michigan	92	9	—	81	60	7	—	78	44

Table G.3—Continued

State	Total number of institutions	Type of Retention Authority							
		Number holding persons not yet arraigned or being held for other authorities				Number holding persons arraigned and awaiting trial			
		Adult			Juvenile	Adult			Juvenile
		Male only	Female only	Male & female		Male only	Female only	Male & female	
Minnesota	77	7	—	67	64	5	—	64	51
Mississippi	98	4	—	90	84	4	1	88	76
Missouri	144	25	—	116	107	24	—	111	90
Montana	68	10	—	57	50	12	—	53	38
Nebraska	99	13	—	84	80	13	—	81	70
Nevada	23	—	—	22	16	—	—	22	15
New Hampshire	11	3	—	8	4	3	—	8	3
New Jersey	32	3	—	26	20	2	—	24	19
New Mexico	44	6	2	40	35	3	—	39	30
New York	75	2	—	55	39	8	2	58	38
North Carolina	100	8	—	96	76	2	—	97	74
North Dakota	50	2	—	42	28	8	—	42	25
Ohio	160	25	—	131	106	25	—	110	72
Oklahoma	112	6	—	105	75	10	—	94	63
Oregon	69	11	—	61	54	9	—	54	34
Pennsylvania	77	7	—	64	55	10	—	63	43
Rhode Island[1]									
South Carolina	111	5	—	60	48	7	—	57	42
South Dakota	60	6	—	54	49	7	—	52	42
Tennessee	116	6	—	101	86	7	—	99	76
Texas	325	22	—	299	249	23	—	266	197
Utah	34	5	—	27	20	2	—	26	15
Vermont	6	1	—	5	2	1	—	3	2
Virginia	96	2	—	87	78	78	2	88	76
Washington	83	17	—	66	41	14	—	63	28
West Virginia	61	7	1	54	50	7	—	52	45
Wisconsin	75	—	—	71	69	—	1	70	63
Wyoming	33	1	—	32	32	1	—	31	28

[1]Jails are not locally administered but rather are operated by the State government.

Table G.4 Jail Employment and Payroll, for the U.S. and by State—March 1970

State	Number of employees			March Payroll			Average earnings of full-time Employees
	Total	Full-time	Part-time	Total	Full-time	Part-time	
U.S. total	33,729	28,053	5,676	$18,094,578	$17,304,828	$789,750	$617
Cities with population of 25,000 or more, and counties	32,288	27,613	4,675	17,788,270	17,120,630	667,640	620
Cities with population under 25,000	1,441	440	1,001	306,308	184,198	122,110	419
Alabama	449	300	149	147,774	131,870	15,904	440
Alaska	43	37	6	24,672	22,474	2,198	607
Arizona	286	232	54	132,371	125,738	6,633	542
Arkansas	229	118	111	52,001	39,902	12,099	338
California	4,623	4,399	224	3,412,541	3,341,719	70,822	760
Colorado	405	302	103	196,490	183,761	12,729	608
Connecticut[1]	—	—	—	—	—	—	—
Delaware[1]	—	—	—	—	—	—	—
District of Columbia	953	941	12	804,890	799,034	5,856	849
Florida	1,517	1,368	149	707,001	685,916	21,085	501
Georgia	1,366	1,059	307	507,419	466,873	40,546	441
Hawaii	74	74		42,408	42,408		573
Idaho	110	38	72	22,413	14,438	7,975	380
Illinois	1,410	1,231	179	808,589	783,558	25,031	637
Indiana	561	446	115	239,125	224,885	14,240	504
Iowa	213	101	112	60,938	49,083	11,855	486
Kansas	271	123	148	71,258	57,458	13,800	467
Kentucky	488	296	192	139,792	118,448	21,344	400
Louisiana	603	504	99	218,270	205,973	12,297	409
Maine	107	67	40	35,790	31,266	4,524	467
Maryland	529	507	22	310,255	306,259	3,996	604
Massachusetts	868	755	113	515,689	493,266	22,423	653
Michigan	1,122	965	157	646,742	619,346	27,396	642
Minnesota	417	294	123	217,293	196,593	20,700	669

Table G.4—Continued

State	Number of employees			March Payroll			Average earnings of full-time Employees
	Total	Full-time	Part-time	Total	Full-time	Part-time	
Mississippi	299	121	178	67,342	48,084	19,258	397
Missouri	644	478	166	254,318	235,287	19,031	492
Montana	122	47	75	30,178	20,706	9,472	441
Nebraska	183	82	101	46,442	35,528	10,914	433
Nevada	127	109	18	60,838	58,688	2,150	538
New Hampshire	113	90	23	41,346	38,317	3,029	426
New Jersey	1,296	1,183	113	826,824	807,256	19,568	682
New Mexico	171	122	49	57,528	50,651	6,877	415
New York	4,698	4,394	304	3,322,731	3,272,167	50,564	745
North Carolina	413	319	94	141,163	129,640	11,523	406
North Dakota	74	18	56	13,224	7,050	6,174	392
Ohio	1,312	1,061	251	610,450	574,943	35,507	542
Oklahoma	349	209	140	111,193	94,070	17,123	450
Oregon	350	234	116	173,863	158,819	15,044	679
Pennsylvania	1,883	1,720	163	1,034,325	1,008,982	25,343	587
Rhode Island[1]	—	—	—	—	—	—	—
South Carolina	679	571	108	229,104	217,125	11,979	380
South Dakota	88	30	58	16,949	10,513	6,436	350
Tennessee	733	527	206	266,288	247,606	18,682	470
Texas	1,463	1,010	453	533,155	476,908	56,247	472
Utah	127	72	55	45,019	38,300	6,719	532
Vermont	7	—	7	960	—	960	—
Virginia	699	618	81	291,521	281,744	9,777	456
Washington	469	334	135	237,017	216,581	20,436	648
West Virginia	200	132	68	56,900	48,719	8,181	369
Wisconsin	514	385	129	291,235	271,340	19,895	705
Wyoming	72	30	42	20,944	15,536	5,408	518

[1]Jails are not locally administered but rather are operated by the State government.

175

Table G.5 Number of Adult Jails Holding Juveniles by Type of Retention, for the United States and by State

State	Total Number of institutions receiving juveniles	Number holding juveniles not yet arraigned or for other authority	Number holding juveniles arraigned and awaiting trial	Number holding convicted juveniles awaiting further legal action	Number holding juveniles serving sentences of one year or less	Number holding juveniles serving sentences of more than one year
U.S. total	2,822	2,785	2,289	856	767	67
Cities with population of 25,000 or more, and counties	2,446	2,411	2,094	822	711	66
Cities with population under 25,000	376	374	195	34	56	1
Alabama	82	82	69	16	12	2
Alaska	4	4	2	2	2	—
Arizona	22	21	17	4	7	—
Arkansas	78	77	62	16	19	1
California	79	77	35	13	15	1
Colorado	58	55	51	23	25	4
Connecticut[1]	—	—	—	—	—	—
Delaware[1]	1	1	1	1	1	—
District of Columbia	77	75	57	24	23	1
Florida	111	109	76	18	11	2
Georgia	2	2	1	—	—	2
Hawaii	—	—	—	—	—	—
Idaho	50	50	42	20	26	2
Illinois	87	86	75	29	30	—
Indiana	87	85	79	33	29	—
Iowa	78	78	65	27	33	1
Kansas	97	95	83	36	35	1
Kentucky	107	103	90	16	17	3
Louisiana	68	68	47	11	12	—
Maine	15	15	13	6	4	—
Maryland	19	19	18	7	8	2
Massachusetts	7	6	7	2	2	—
Michigan	61	60	44	23	24	—

Table G.5—Continued

State	Total Number of institutions receiving juveniles	Number holding juveniles not yet arraigned or for other authority	Number holding juveniles arraigned and awaiting trial	Number holding convicted juveniles awaiting further legal action	Number holding juveniles serving sentences of one year or less	Number holding juveniles serving sentences of more than one year
Minnesota	66	64	51	26	19	—
Mississippi	85	84	76	16	15	2
Missouri	107	107	90	42	31	2
Montana	50	50	38	23	22	1
Nebraska	80	80	70	36	31	—
Nevada	16	16	15	7	3	—
New Hampshire	4	4	3	—	—	—
New Jersey	20	20	19	11	4	—
New Mexico	36	35	30	8	6	—
New York	44	39	38	25	31	4
North Carolina	77	76	74	18	5	1
North Dakota	28	28	25	7	8	—
Ohio	106	106	72	30	35	—
Oklahoma	75	75	63	19	20	1
Oregon	54	54	34	17	17	—
Pennsylvania	55	55	43	13	14	8
Rhode Island[1]	—	—	—	—	—	—
South Carolina	48	48	42	8	4	—
South Dakota	49	49	42	21	14	1
Tennessee	87	86	76	8	8	2
Texas	250	249	197	63	44	21
Utah	20	20	15	3	4	1
Vermont	2	2	2	1	—	—
Virginia	81	78	76	41	28	1
Washington	41	41	28	11	9	—
West Virginia	50	50	45	18	9	—
Wisconsin	69	69	63	43	35	—
Wyoming	32	32	28	14	16	—

[1] Jails are not locally administered but rather are operated by the State government.

Table G.6 Number of Jails by Extent of Overcrowding of Inmates, for the United States and by State—March 1970

State	Total number of institutions	Number with more inmates than design capacity	Percent over capacity	Number of jails exceeding capacity by—					
				Less than 5 persons	5-9 persons	10-24 persons	25-99 persons	100-299 persons	300 or more persons
U.S. total	4,037	205	5.1	57	35	35	47	17	14
Alabama	107	1	0.9	—	1	1	—	—	—
Alaska	8	1	12.5	1	1	1	1	—	—
Arizona	39	4	10.3	2	2	—	1	—	—
Arkansas	110	5	4.6	5	—	2	3	—	—
California	166	21	12.7	1	3	3	5	4	1
Colorado	78	1	1.3	1	—	—	—	—	—
Connecticut[1]	—	—	—	—	—	—	—	—	—
Delaware[1]	—	—	—	—	—	—	—	—	—
District of Columbia	5	2	40.0	—	—	—	—	2	—
Florida	167	10	6.0	3	—	2	3	2	1
Georgia	240	7	2.9	1	3	1	2	—	—
Hawaii	4	—	—	—	—	—	—	—	—
Idaho	61	2	3.3	2	—	—	—	—	—
Illinois	108	4	3.7	2	2	1	—	—	1
Indiana	97	6	6.2	2	2	—	2	—	—
Iowa	93	2	1.6	—	—	—	—	—	—
Kansas	123	2	7.4	9	2	2	—	—	—
Kentucky	148	11	9.5	2	1	—	—	—	—
Louisiana	95	9		—	1	33	2	—	1
Maine	16	—	—	—	—	—	—	—	—
Maryland	23	4	17.4	—	1	—	3	—	—
Massachusetts	18	2	11.1	—	1	—	1	—	—
Michigan	92	7	7.6	—	4	—	—	—	—
Minnesota	77	1	1.3	1	—	—	—	2	—
Mississippi	98	2	2.0	—	1	1	—	—	—

Table G.6—Continued

State	Total number of institutions	Number with more inmates than design capacity	Percent over capacity	Number of jails exceeding capacity by—					
				Less than 5 persons	5-9 persons	10-24 persons	25-99 persons	100-299 persons	300 or more persons
Missouri	144	5	3.5	1	1	2	1	—	—
Montana	68	1	1.5	1	—	—	—	—	—
Nebraska	99	3	3.0	2	—	—	1	—	—
Nevada	23	2	8.7	—	2	—	—	—	—
New Hampshire	11	—	—	—	—	—	—	—	—
New Jersey	32	8	25.0	—	—	—	4	4	—
New Mexico	44	3	6.8	1	1	1	—	—	—
New York	75	15	20.0	1	1	2	3	1	7
North Carolina	100	4	4.0	3	1	—	—	—	—
North Dakota	50	—	—	—	—	—	—	—	—
Ohio	160	10	6.3	3	2	2	2	1	—
Oklahoma	112	5	4.5	1	2	1	1	—	—
Oregon	69	4	5.8	2	1	—	—	—	1
Pennsylvania	77	7	9.1	1	1	1	3	1	—
Rhode Island[1]	—	—	—	—	—	—	—	—	—
South Carolina	111	4	3.6	1	1	1	1	—	—
South Dakota	60	1	1.7	1	—	—	—	—	—
Tennessee	116	5	4.3	1	—	3	—	1	—
Texas	325	17	5.2	5	—	6	3	1	2
Utah	34	1	2.9	1	—	—	—	—	—
Vermont	6	—	—	—	—	—	—	—	—
Virginia	96	5	5.2	2	—	—	3	—	—
Washington	83	—	—	—	—	—	—	—	—
West Virginia	61	1	1.6	—	1	—	—	—	—
Wisconsin	75	1	1.3	1	—	—	—	—	—
Wyoming	33	1	3.0	1	—	—	—	—	—

[1] Jails are not locally administered but rather are operated by the State government.

Table G.7 Number and Percent of Cells in City (Over 25,000 Population) and County Jails, by Age of Cell, for the United States and by State — March 1970

State	Total number of institutions	Total number of cells	Cells 1 day to 25 years old		Cells 26–50 years old		Cells 51–75 years old		Cells 76–100 years old		Cells Over 100 years old	
			Number	Percent	Number	Percent	Number	Percent	Number	Percent	Number	Percent
Total	3,319	97,891	42,883	43.8	30,390	31.0	12,706	13.0	6,496	6.6	5,416	5.5
Alabama	80	2,616	1,527	58.4	943	36.0	51	1.9	15	0.6	80	3.1
Alaska	2	57	57	100.0	—	—	—	—	—	—	—	—
Arizona	17	436	219	50.2	140	32.1	77	17.7	—	—	—	—
Arkansas	81	912	217	23.8	563	61.7	122	13.4	10	1.1	—	—
California	134	7,858	6,030	76.7	1,692	21.5	125	1.6	11	0.1	—	—
Colorado	61	1,189	773	65.0	233	19.6	82	6.9	101	8.5	—	—
Connecticut[1]	—	—	—	—	—	—	—	—	—	—	—	—
Delaware[1]	—	—	—	—	—	—	—	—	—	—	—	—
District of Columbia	5	1,150	345	30.0	531	46.2	—	—	274	23.8	—	—
Florida	101	2,744	2,242	81.7	350	12.8	79	2.9	73	2.7	—	—
Georgia	205	3,506	1,621	46.2	1,081	30.8	509	14.5	116	3.3	179	5.1
Hawaii	4	90	44	48.9	28	31.1	18	20.0	—	—	—	—
Idaho	44	387	77	19.9	245	63.3	60	15.5	5	1.3	—	—
Illinois	103	3,974	728	18.3	1,599	40.2	1,146	28.8	378	9.5	123	3.1
Indiana	94	2,358	1,027	43.6	253	10.7	228	9.7	694	29.4	156	6.6
Iowa	89	1,005	229	22.8	353	35.1	300	29.9	88	8.8	35	3.5
Kansas	108	1,304	683	52.4	400	30.7	178	13.7	43	3.3	—	—
Kentucky	122	1,996	499	25.0	459	23.0	421	21.1	285	14.3	332	16.6
Louisiana	72	2,097	1,235	58.9	725	34.6	123	5.9	14	0.7	—	—
Maine	14	381	71	18.6	50	13.1	38	10.0	51	13.4	171	44.9
Maryland	23	1,219	920	75.5	54	4.4	86	7.1	111	9.1	48	3.9
Massachusetts	18	2,861	245	8.6	384	13.4	716	25.0	435	15.2	1,081	37.8
Michigan	90	2,458	1,415	57.6	892	36.3	48	2.0	103	4.2	—	—
Minnesota	70	1,793	528	29.4	659	36.8	469	26.2	137	7.6	—	—
Mississippi	91	1,362	659	48.4	443	32.5	160	11.7	68	5.0	32	2.3

Table G.7—Continued

State	Total number of institutions	Total number of cells	Cells 1 day to 25 years old		Cells 26–50 years old		Cells 51–75 years old		Cells 76–100 years old		Cells Over 100 years old	
			Number	Percent	Number	Percent	Number	Percent	Number	Percent	Number	Percent
Missouri	113	2,411	942	39.1	897	37.2	470	19.5	57	2.4	45	1.9
Montana	54	617	89	14.4	187	30.3	233	37.8	108	17.5	—	—
Nebraska	82	736	221	30.0	212	28.8	266	36.1	35	4.8	2	0.3
Nevada	19	372	253	68.0	20	5.4	82	22.0	17	4.6	—	—
New Hampshire	11	286	18	6.3	16	5.6	138	48.3	72	25.2	42	14.7
New Jersey	31	3,092	467	15.1	1,382	44.7	644	20.8	274	8.9	325	10.5
New Mexico	32	669	224	33.5	374	55.9	71	10.6	—	—	—	—
New York	74	13,119	5,504	42.0	6,050	46.1	1,214	9.3	271	2.1	80	0.6
North Carolina	96	2,466	1,091	44.2	864	35.0	436	17.7	51	2.1	24	1.0
North Dakota	45	380	110	28.9	98	25.8	172	45.3	—	—	—	—
Ohio	112	4,206	1,360	32.3	778	18.5	428	10.2	657	15.6	983	23.4
Oklahoma	82	1,235	362	29.3	597	48.3	259	21.0	8	0.6	9	0.7
Oregon	35	615	232	37.7	256	41.6	121	19.7	6	1.0	—	—
Pennsylvania	73	6,569	1,034	15.7	1,545	23.5	1,206	18.4	1,261	19.2	1,523	23.2
Rhode Island[1]	—	—	—	—	—	—	—	—	—	—	—	—
South Carolina	101	1,637	895	54.7	449	27.4	239	14.6	34	2.1	20	1.2
South Dakota	47	324	104	32.1	100	30.9	99	30.6	21	6.5	—	—
Tennessee	104	1,751	761	43.5	653	37.3	147	8.4	152	8.7	38	2.2
Texas	265	5,690	3,117	54.8	1,794	31.5	568	10.0	211	3.7	—	—
Utah	26	316	207	65.5	94	29.7	15	4.7	—	—	—	—
Vermont	5	57	—	—	16	28.1	19	33.3	10	17.5	12	21.1
Virginia	89	3,054	2,286	74.9	454	14.9	198	6.5	41	1.3	75	2.5
Washington	42	1,026	456	44.4	454	44.2	116	11.3	—	—	—	—
West Virginia	57	1,267	275	21.7	547	43.2	295	23.3	149	11.8	1	0.1
Wisconsin	75	1,973	1,394	70.7	372	18.9	158	8.0	49	2.5	—	—
Wyoming	21	270	90	33.3	104	38.5	76	28.1	—	—	—	—

[1]Jails are not locally administered but rather are operated by the State government.

181

Table G.8 Number and Percent of City (Over 25,000 Population) and County Jails With and Without Selected Facilities, for the United States and by State

State	Total number of institutions	Recreational facilities Without Number	Without Percent	With Number	With Percent	Educational facilities Without Number	Without Percent	With Number	With Percent
Total	3,319	2,869	86.4	450	13.6	2,961	89.2	358	10.8
Alabama	80	76	95.0	4	5.0	78	97.5	—	—
Alaska	2	—	—	2	100.0	2	100.0	—	—
Arizona	17	17	100.0	—	—	15	88.2	2	11.8
Arkansas	81	77	95.1	4	4.9	78	96.3	3	3.7
California	134	63	47.0	71	53.0	95	70.9	39	29.1
Colorado	61	53	86.9	8	13.1	56	91.8	5	8.2
Connecticut[1]	—	—	—	—	—	—	—	—	—
Delaware[1]	—	—	—	—	—	—	—	—	—
District of Columbia	5	1	20.0	4	80.0	—	—	5	100.0
Florida	101	76	75.2	25	24.8	89	88.1	12	11.9
Georgia	205	163	79.5	42	20.5	170	82.9	35	17.1
Hawaii	4	2	50.0	2	50.0	3	75.0	1	25.0
Idaho	44	43	97.7	1	2.3	44	100.0	—	—
Illinois	103	97	94.2	6	5.8	97	94.2	6	5.8
Indiana	94	87	92.6	7	7.4	90	95.7	4	4.3
Iowa	89	79	88.8	10	11.2	80	89.9	9	10.1
Kansas	108	104	96.3	4	3.7	102	94.4	6	5.6
Kentucky	122	116	95.1	6	4.9	118	96.7	4	3.3
Louisiana	72	61	84.7	11	15.3	63	87.5	9	12.5
Maine	14	9	64.3	5	35.7	13	92.9	1	7.1
Maryland	23	18	78.3	5	21.7	17	73.9	6	26.1
Massachusetts	18	4	22.2	14	77.8	5	27.8	13	72.2
Michigan	90	81	90.0	9	10.0	76	84.4	14	15.6
Minnesota	70	60	85.7	10	14.3	60	85.7	10	14.3
Mississippi	91	90	98.9	1	1.1	90	98.9	1	1.1
Missouri	113	105	92.9	8	7.1	103	91.2	10	8.8

182

Table G.8—Continued

State	Total number of institutions	Recreational facilities				Educational facilities			
		Without		With		Without		With	
		Number	Percent	Number	Percent	Number	Percent	Number	Percent
Montana	54	53	98.1	1	1.9	54	100.0	—	—
Nebraska	82	72	87.8	10	12.2	78	95.1	4	4.9
Nevada	19	18	94.7	1	5.3	19	100.0	—	—
New Hampshire	11	5	45.5	6	54.5	7	63.6	4	36.4
New Jersey	31	21	67.7	10	32.3	15	48.4	16	51.6
New Mexico	32	30	93.8	2	6.2	30	93.8	2	6.2
New York	74	30	40.5	44	59.5	35	47.3	39	52.7
North Carolina	96	91	94.8	5	5.2	90	93.7	6	6.3
North Dakota	45	42	93.3	3	6.7	41	91.1	4	8.9
Ohio	112	103	92.0	9	8.0	109	97.3	3	2.7
Oklahoma	82	77	93.9	5	6.1	80	97.6	2	2.4
Oregon	35	32	91.4	3	8.6	30	85.7	5	14.3
Pennsylvania	73	38	52.1	35	47.9	49	67.1	24	32.9
Rhode Island[1]		—	—	—	—	—	—	—	—
South Carolina	101	86	85.1	15	14.9	91	90.1	10	9.9
South Dakota	47	43	91.5	4	8.5	43	91.5	4	8.5
Tennessee	104	98	94.2	6	5.8	99	95.2	5	4.8
Texas	265	258	97.4	7	2.6	257	97.0	8	3.0
Utah	26	24	92.3	2	7.7	24	92.3	2	7.7
Vermont	5	5	100.0	—	—	5	100.0	—	—
Virginia	89	82	92.1	7	7.9	83	93.3	6	6.7
Washington	42	38	90.5	4	9.5	36	85.7	6	14.3
West Virginia	57	55	96.5	2	3.5	56	98.2	1	1.8
Wisconsin	75	66	88.0	9	12.0	66	88.0	9	12.0
Wyoming	21	'20	95.2	1	4.8	20	95.2	1	4.8

[1] Jails are not locally administered but rather are operated by the State government.

183

Appendix H
Rules for the Guidance of Inmates— County Jail

Jail Rules
For the Guidance of Inmates—County Jail

THE FOLLOWING RULES WILL GOVERN THE CONDUCT OF THE INMATES OF THE COUNTY JAIL AND FOR THE GOOD OF ALL SHOULD BE COMPLIED WITH TO THE FULLEST EXTENT

1. ALL PRISONERS, on being booked in, will be given two clean blankets, one mattress and one towel. These articles will be checked out upon prisoner's release. Any damage to bedding or jail garments will be charged against prisoner's funds.

2. ALL PRISONERS will be awakened at 6:00 A.M. and will be expected to make up beds.

3. Soap and water are cheap. ALL PRISONERS are requested to take a bath at once and if any bugs are present or suspected, ask for DDT powder at once.

4. The services of the County Doctor are available for any who have a REAL ailment. Please do not ask for the doctor otherwise as he is a very busy man.

5. Books and reading material will be provided, but only as long as I have the cooperation of the inmates of this jail. Any failure to cooperate will result in withdrawal of these privileges.

6. Visiting hours will be 1:00 to 4:00 on Saturdays and Sundays. Advise those who may be visiting you of these hours as there will be

Reprinted from "Bureau of Prisons Rules," mimeographed (Washington, D.C.: U.S. Department of Justice, n.d.).

185

no exceptions. Tuesday visiting hours for friends who are approved is from 5:30 to 7:30 P.M.

7. You may write up to one letter per day, not to exceed two double pages, written in a normal, legible handwriting. All mail must have a return name and address, incoming and outgoing.

8. Commissary may be purchased on assigned days. Orders limited to eight (8) packages cigarettes, 5 candy bars, toothbrush and comb. No articles in either glass or tin containers will be purchased. The following items will be accepted over the counter for prisoners: clothing and cash.

9. Day rooms and cells must be cleaned out daily. Strings tied to bars of cell or papers between bars will not be tolerated. *Cigarette butts must be kept off the floors* and beds must be neatly made.

10. *Any loud singing or whistling or unnecessary noise will not be tolerated.*

11. Remember you are in jail. We did not invite you here but will try to fulfill our duty while you are here, by making things as pleasant as possible. This is largely dependent upon you as inmates being cooperative and willing to do your share toward this end.

12. Any just complaints will be heard and considered by me and should be directed through the Jail Division Captain.

13. Cells and cell blocks will be ready for inspection by 10:00 A.M. each morning.

14. Any person on Parole or Probation from any County or Penal Institution will not be permitted to visit this jail. This also includes former inmates from any institution.

15. ANY VIOLATIONS OF THESE RULES WILL RESULT IN RESTRICTION OF PRIVILEGES INCLUDING VISITING, COMMISSARY OR T.V.

Notes

Chapter 2

1. Black's *Law Dictionary* defines blood feud as "Avenging the slaughter of kin on the person who slaughtered him or on his belongings. Whether the teutonic or the Anglo-Saxon law had a legal right of blood-feud has been disputed, but in Alfred's day it was unlawful to begin a feud until an attempt had been made to exact the price of the life."

2. Clarence R. Jeffery, "The Development of Crime in Early English Society," in William J. Chambless (ed.), *Crime and the Legal Process* (New York: McGraw-Hill Book Company, 1969), p. 20.

3. Ibid.

4. Thomas F. Adams, *Introduction to the Administration of Justice* (Englewood Cliffs, N.J.: Prentice-Hall, 1975), p. 101.

5. Edith E. Flynn, "Jails and Criminal Justice," in Lloyd E. Ohlin (ed.), *Prisoners in America* (Englewood Cliffs, N.J.: Prentice-Hall, 1973), p. 50.

6. Adams, *Administration of Justice*, p. 101.

7. Ibid., p. 102.

8. Ibid.

9. Robert G. Caldwell, *Criminology* (New York: The Roland Press, 1965), p. 491.

10. There were English jails in existence before this time but unfortunately the exact dates are not available. Jails may easily predate Henry II by as much as two hundred years. See Ralph B. Pugh, *Imprisonment in Medieval England* (Cambridge: At the University Press, 1968), and George Ives, *A History of Penal Methods* (1914; reprint ed., Montclair, N.J.: Patterson Smith, 1970).

11. The assize was the king's superior court held periodically in each county. Clarendon was the geographical location of one assize.

12. *History of the English Law*, vol. 2, 2d ed. (Boston: Little, Brown, 1903), p. 516; quoted in Louis N. Robinson, *Penology in the United States* (Philadelphia: John C. Winston Co., 1922), p. 33.

13. Richard R. Korn and Lloyd W. McCorkle, *Criminology and Penology* (New York: Holt, Rinehart, and Winston, 1967), p. 406.

14. Adams, *Administration of Justice*, p. 102.
15. A. M. Kirkpatrick, "Jails in Historical Perspective," *Canadian Journal of Corrections* 6 (October 1964): 406.

Chapter 3

1. Louis N. Robinson, *Penology in the United States* (Philadelphia: The John C. Winston Company, 1922).
2. See A. M. Kirkpatrick, "Jails in Historical Perspective," *Canadian Journal of Corrections* 6 (October 1974): 406. The site was at the legendary St. Brides Well. This name, which was later corrupted to *Bridewell*, became the term used to identify all English houses of correction.
3. Robinson, *Penology*, p. 59.
4. Ibid., p. 58.
5. Ibid., pp. 34–35.
6. E. M. Leonard, *The Early History of English Poor Relief* (Cambridge: University Press, 1900), pp. 220–21.
7. Richard R. Korn and Lloyd W. McCorkle, *Criminology and Penology* (New York: Holt, Rinehart, and Winston, 1967), p. 409.
8. Max Grunhut, *Penal Reform* (New York: The Clarendon Press, 1948), p. 29.
9. Korn and McCorkle, *Criminology and Penology*, p. 410
10. Elmer J. Johnson, *Crime, Correction and Society,* rev. ed. (Homewood, Ill.; Dorsey Press, 1968), p. 491.
11. Robert G. Caldwell, *Criminology* (New York: Ronald Press Co., 1965), p. 494.
12. Kirkpatrick, "Jails in Historical Perspective," p. 407.
13. Ibid.

Chapter 4

1. Carl Bridenbaugh, *Cities in the Wilderness: Urban Life in America 1625–1742* (New York: Capricorn Books, 1964), pp. 68–71.
2. Louis N. Robinson, *Penology in the United States* (Philadelphia: John C. Winston, 1922), p. 36.
3. The first jail constructed in America was built in Virginia at the time of the establishment of the colony at Jamestown. It was authorized in the "articles, instructions and orders" issued by James I on November 20, 1606. There is no available record as to the date the jail was actually built, but there are records of the imprisonment in it of

several Indians in 1608 and of a young German in 1609. See Frank W. Hoffer, Delbert M. Mann, and Floyd N. House, *The Jails of Virginia* (New York: D. Appleton-Century Company, 1933), pp. 13–29.

4. Bridenbaugh, *Cities in the Wilderness,* p. 74.

5. Ibid.

6. David J. Rothman, *The Discovery of the Asylum* (Boston: Little, Brown, 1971), p. 55.

7. Another early jail still in existence is the one located in York Village, Maine. It was constructed in 1653. The Williamsburg jail was an exception to the jails of the time. Physically it was a much cleaner jail, and it appears there was more care and humanity displayed in handling the prisoners.

8. For a description of the old jail see Marcus Whiffen, *The Public Buildings of Williamsburg* (Williamsburg, Va.: Colonial Williamsburg, Inc. 1958).

9. There were advantages and disadvantages of having a primitive toilet of this type. It was advantageous to have the instant disposal of waste and not to have to use buckets. The main disadvantage was that these toilets were unhealthy and undoubtedly a source of disease.

10. Robinson, *Penology,* p. 60.

Chapter 5

1. The terms *prison* and *penitentiary* are used synonymously. The term *penitentiary* was coined by John Howard and derived from the word *penitence* (a lawbreaker could atone for his crime and sin by penance). The word *prison* was sometimes used to denote county and city jails. Although this chapter is concerned with the development of state prisons, we will find that in the next chapter "prisons" may refer to local, short-term facilities.

2. For example, in the colony of Virginia many individuals were spared a death penalty on their second, third, and even fourth convictions and/or trials. Life was considered with much reverence, and the matter of the death penalty was not taken lightly. (From a conversation with Richard H. Carter of The Colonial Williamsburg Foundation).

3. Robert G. Caldwell, *Criminology* (New York: Ronald Press, 1965), p. 495.

4. Ibid., p. 502.

5. Elmer H. Johnson, *Crime, Correction and Society* (Homewood, Ill.: Dorsey Press, 1974), p. 482.

6. Caldwell, *Criminology*, p. 503. The prisons had a much wider function in that they satisfied the often talked-about need that society has of revenge, retribution, and deterrence.
7. Caldwell, *Criminology*, p. 503.
8. Harry E. Allen and Clifford E. Simonsen, *Corrections in America* (Beverly Hills: Glencoe Press, 1975), p. 29.
9. Caldwell, *Criminology*, p. 504. For a good description of the Walnut Street Jail see Negley K. Teeters, *The Cradle of the Penitentiary* (Philadelphia: Pennsylvania Prison Society, 1955).
10. Although the Walnut Street Jail is considered the first prison, it should be pointed out that there was an unsuccessful attempt at developing a prison in an abandoned copper mine at Simsbury, Connecticut. Known as the Newgate Prison, it predated the Walnut Street Jail by several years.
11. Bentham's panoptican was planned as a large structure covered by a glass case. The central cupola would let guards see into all cells. The cells were located in a circular arrangement like spokes on a wheel. This type of prison was not constructed during Bentham's life. See Allen and Simonsen, *Corrections*, p. 32.
12. Caldwell, *Criminology*, p. 507.
13. Richard R. Korn and Lloyd W. McCorkle, *Criminology and Penology* (New York: Holt, Rinehart, and Winston, 1967), p. 413.
14. Ibid.
15. Caldwell, *Criminology*, p. 509.
16. Ibid.

Chapter 6

1. Harry E. Barnes, *The Story of Punishment* (Boston: The Stratford Co., 1930), pp. 192–93.
2. There is a differentiation between changes in conditions and changes in function in regard to jails. When we speak of changes in conditions we are referring to the physical and mental lot of the inmates. Thus a change in conditions would indicate that from an inmate's perspective things were better or worse. When we speak of changes in function we are referring more to the role of the jail. Thus a change in function, such as eliminating debtors from incarceration, indicates a different role for the jail. Changes in either function or condition may have an effect upon the other.
3. *The 5th Annual Report of the Board of Managers of the Prison Discipline Society* (Boston, 1830; reprint ed., Montclair, N.J.: Patterson Smith, 1972), p. 43. These reports will hereafter be referred to as the *Prison Discipline Society*.

4. See for example, Anthony M. Platt, *The Child Savers* (Chicago: University of Chicago Press, 1969); Robert M. Mennel, *Thorns and Thistles* (Hanover, N.H.: University Press of New England, 1973); and Gustave de Beaumont and Alexis de Tocqueville, *On the Penitentiary System in the United States and Its Application in France* (reprint ed., Carbondale: Southern Illinois University Press, 1964).

5. Robert G. Caldwell, *Criminology* (New York: Ronald Press, 1965), p. 510.

6. See Mennel, *Thorns and Thistles,* for more information on this general topic.

7. Ibid., p. 57.

8. The reprints of the Prison Discipline Society reports are bound into six volumes by Patterson Smith, 1972.

9. *Prison Discipline Society Report 2,* 1827, p. 89.

10. *Prison Discipline Society Report 9,* 1834, pp. 11–13.

11. *Prison Discipline Society Report 12,* 1837, p. 64.

12. Ibid., pp. 66–68.

13. *Prison Discipline Society Report 16,* 1841, pp. 56–60.

14. Jesse F. Steiner and Roy M. Brown, *The North Carolina Chain Gang* (Chapel Hill: University of North Carolina Press, 1927), p. 12.

15. Continual examples of this are cited in Steiner and Brown, *North Carolina Chain Gang.*

16. Joseph F. Fishman, *Crucibles of Crime* (New York: Cosmopolis Press, 1923), p. 142.

17. Ibid.

18. Most of the cellular construction was first developed with the prisons. This type of construction became more prominent in the jails after the prison movement began.

19. J. M. Moynahan, *Corrections in the County City Jail—Spokane, Washington* (Spokane, Wash.: Rehabilitative Services Program, 1974), p. 7.

20. Moynahan, *Corrections,* p. 7.

21. For an explanation of type of jail, see Ronald Goldfarb, *Jails: The Ultimate Ghetto of the Criminal Justice System* (Garden City, N.Y.: Doubleday, Anchor, 1975), p. 12; and Fishman, *Crucibles of Crime,* pp. 49-50.

22. From a conversation with Mary H. Oakey (October 1976), who is writing a history of the jails in Washington, D.C.

23. See Fishman, *Crucibles of Crime*; Steiner and Brown, *North Carolina Chain Gang*; and David J. Rothman, *The Discovery of the Asylum* (Boston: Little, Brown, 1971).

Chapter 7

1. Charles R. Henderson, ed., *Penology and Reformatory Institutions* (New York: Charities Publication Committee, 1900), p. 24.
2. Joseph F. Fishman, *Crucibles of Crime* (New York: Cosmopolis Press, 1923), pp. 240–44.
3. Hastings H. Hart, "Police Jails and Village Lockups" in *Report on Penal Institutions, Probation and Parole No. 9* (Washington, D.C.: National Commission on Law Observance and Enforcement, 1931), pp. 330-32.
4. Much of the literature of the time cited ways of eliminating many of the "evils" associated with jails. For example, see Fishman, *Crucibles of Crime*, pp. 250–99.
5. Hart, "Police Jails," pp. 342–43.
6. One such organization is found in the state of Washington. For the constitution of this organization, see Appendix F, Constitution of the Washington State Jailers Association.
7. This basic course was designed and is administered by Jake Parker under the direction of the Washington State Criminal Justice Training Commission. Serving as a basic course, this eighty-hour class is designed for personnel employed in the state's confinement institutions.
8. Fishman, *Crucibles of Crime*, p. 84.
9. In personal discussions, Capt. E. Byron Franz, the past superintendent of the Spokane County-City Jail, has indicated that he feels very strongly that the jail programs have helped prevent major riots and a great deal of general unrest. He attributed this to the fact that inmates are busy and able to verbally vent their frustrations.
10. To date there is not an adequate text aimed at treatment programs as such. However, see Charles L. Newman et al., *Local Jails and Drug Treatment* (University Park: Pennsylvania State University, 1976); National Association of Counties, "Jail Inmate Rehabilitation Program," *American County* 37, no. 10 (1972): 11–12; *Jail Programs* (Washington, D.C.: The National Sheriffs Association, 1972); and J. M. Moynahan, *Corrections in the County-City Jail, Spokane, Washington* (Spokane, Wash.: Rehabilitative Services Program, 1974).

Chapter 8

1. Earlier census reports have cited the number of inmates held in facilities in the United States but have in no way been as detailed as this project.
2. Jails were defined as "Any individual facility operated by a unit of local government (that is, a municipality or township with a 1960 population of 1,000 or more persons, or a county) for the detention or

correction of adults suspected or convicted of a crime. Hospitals for the criminally insane are not included. Detention authority is defined as a minimum of 48 hours duration. The lower limit of 1,000 population for cities and townships was set because very few places smaller than this have jails which hold persons for 48 hours or more. In the course of the census, no townships of any size were identified which had jails meeting the 48-hours criterion." *National Jail Census 1970* (Washington, D.C.: Law Enforcement Assistance Admininstration, U.S. Department of Justice, 1971), pp. 6–7.

3. "Selected facilities" in the Census referred to "The availability of recreational and educational facilities and/or programs of any kind; the availability of medical facilities of any type; the availability of a visiting room, including an attorney's consultation room; and the availability of operating flush toilets." *National Jail Census 1970*, p. 7.

4. Hart's project was the most ambitious study up to that time. There were earlier reports which just cited conditions in certain states but there had been no national survey. See Appendix C, Police Jails and Village Lockups.

5. The materials in the remainder of this chapter are from *National Jail Census 1970*.

6. With regard to juveniles the report stated: "The legal definitions and age limits of juveniles vary by state. The responding official completing the questionnaire in each jurisdiction was asked to apply the definitions appropriate to his State in supplying data on the number of juvenile inmates. Not only does the maximum age at which a person may have his case heard in a juvenile court vary by state, but within states it may vary by sex or by offense. In some states there exists a third category falling between juveniles and adults—that of the 'youthful offender' or 'minor.' Generally, this class is considered adult insofar as criminal prosecution is concerned. It should be noted in this regard that in New York, minors (offenders 16-21 years old) are housed separately by law but sometimes within institutions housing those over 21. In the jail census, some institutions in New York reported minors as juveniles and some reported them as adults. Thus the number of 'juveniles' appears very large in two New York City jails which actually hold large numbers of minors." *National Jail Census 1970*, p. 7.

7. The design capacity was defined as, "The number of persons the facility was designed to hold; not included are the arrangements for the accommodation of overcrowding." And the inmate population was said to be, "The number of persons confined in local jails on March 15, 1970." *National Jail Census 1970*, p. 7.

8. Those that were not formally arraigned constituted "persons in jail who had not yet been formally charged before a court." While convicted prisoners awaiting further legal action included "prisoners

awaiting sentencing or under appeal." *National Jail Census 1970,* p. 7.

9. The number of full-time equivalent employees was defined as, "the total number of employees adjusted by applying average fulltime earning rates." *National Jail Census 1970,* p. 7.

10. The operating costs include, "salaries, wages, purchase of supplies, utilities, and transportation, but does not include capital expenditures, such as construction and the purchase of land and equipment." The construction expenditure involves, "Capital outlay for structural additions, replacement facilities, and major alterations, including design, site improvement, and provision of facilities that are an integral part of a structure." *National Jail Census 1970,* p. 7.

Bibliography

Abbott, Edith. *The Real Jail Problem.* Chicago: Juvenile Protective Association, about 1915.

Adams, Thomas F. *Introduction to the Administration of Justice.* Englewood Cliffs, N.J.: Prentice-Hall, 1975.

Adams, Thomas F.; Buck, Gerald; and Hallstrom, Don. *Criminal Justice: Organization and Management.* Pacific Palisades, Calif.: Goodyear Publishing Co., 1974.

Advisory Committee for Adult Detention. *San Francisco Adult Detention Facilities.* San Francisco: Advisory Committee for Adult Detention, 1968.

Alachua County Sheriff's Office. *Establishing Helping Services in Local Jails.* Gainesville, Fla.: Alachua County Sheriff's Office, 1969.

Alexander, Myrl. "Federal Jail Inspection." *Prison Journal* 31, no. 2 (October 1956): 7–9.

Alexander, Myrl. *Jail Administration.* Springfield, Ill.: Charles C. Thomas, 1957.

Allen, Harry E., and Simonsen, Clifford E. *Corrections in America: An Introduction.* Beverly Hills, Calif.: Glencoe Press, 1975.

Alper, Benedict S. *Prisons Inside-Out: Alternatives in Correctional Reform.* Cambridge, Mass.: Ballinger Publishing Co., 1974.

American Bar Association. Commission on Correctional Facilities. *Medical and Health Care in Jails, Prisons, and Other Correctional Facilities.* Washington, D.C.: American Bar Association, 1974.

American Bar Association. Commission on Correctional Facilities. *Survey and Handbook on State Standards and Inspection Legislation for Jails and Juvenile Detention Facilities.* Washington, D.C.: American Bar Association, 1974.

American Civil Liberties Union. *The Seeds of Anguish: An ACLU Study of the D. C. Jail.* Washington, D.C.: American Civil Liberties Union, 1972.

American Correctional Association. *Manual of Correctional Standards* (3rd ed.) Washington, D.C.: American Correctional Association, 1966.

American Foundation. *The County Jail and Related Criminal Justice Services: Polk County, Florida.* Philadelphia: American Foundation, 1970.

Amir, Menachem. "Sociological Study of the House of Correction." *American Journal of Correction* 28, no. 2 (March–April 1966): 20–24.

Amrine, Milton F. "The Future of the Jail in The Light of Modern Trends." *Proceedings of the Sixty-Fifth Annual Congress of the American Prison Association,* (October 1935): 314–21.

Anderson, H. Dewey, and Davidson, Percy E. "A Comparison of County Jail Inmates with the Working Community from Which They Came." *Journal of Criminal Law and Criminology* 28, no. 2: 239–48.

Andry, R. G. *The Short-Term Prisoner.* London: Stevens and Sons, 1963.

Angel, Arthur R., et al. "Preventive Detention: An Empirical Analysis." *Harvard Civil Rights—Civil Liberties Law Review* 6 (March 1971): 303–4.

Arnot, Marie. *For Better or Worse? Nebraska's Misdemeanant Correctional System.* Lincoln, Neb.: Economic Development Department, 1970.

Ashman, Allen, et al. *Lockup: North Carolina at Its Local Jails.* Chapel Hill: University of North Carolina Press, 1969.

Babington, Anthony. *The English Bastille.* London: Macdonald and Company, 1971.

Barnes, Harry E. *The Evolution of Penology in Pennsylvania.* Indianapolis: Bobbs-Merrill, 1927.

Barnes, Harry E. *The Story of Punishment.* Boston: Stratford, 1930. (Chapter 7.)

Barnes, Harry E., and Teeters, Negley K. *New Horizons in Criminology.* Englewood Cliffs, N.J.: Prentice-Hall, 1959. Chapter 24.

Bartholomew, Carole. *Work Release for Misdemeanants in Minnesota.* St. Paul: Minnesota Corrections Department, 1970.

Bases, Nan C., and McDonald, William F. *Preventive Detention in the District of Columbia: the First Ten Months.* Washington, D.C.: Georgetown Institute of Criminal Law Procedure, 1972.

Bates, Sanford. "How Many Years?". *Journal of Criminal Law and Criminology* 19, no. 1 (January 1973): 15–18.

Bates, Sanford. *Prisons and Beyond.* New York: Macmillan, 1936. (Chapter 3.)

Bay Area Social Planning Council. *Alternatives to Incarceration and Proposed Improvements in the Jail System in Contra Costa County.* Oakland, Calif.: Bay Area Social Planning Council, 1972.

Bay Area Social Planning Council. *Report on Community Services for Inmates of the San Mateo Jail and Honor Camps.* Oakland: Bay Area Social Planning Council, 1967.

Beaumont, Gustave de, and Tocqueville, Alexis de. *On the Penitentiary System in the United States and Its Application in France.* 1833. Reprint: Carbondale: Southern Illinois University Press, 1964.

Bennett, J. V. "It's a Crime to Use the Jail." *Of Prisons and Justice.* Washington, D.C.: U.S. Government Printing Office, 1964. Pp. 31–36.

Benton, F. Warren, and Obenland, Robert. *Prison and Jail Security.* Urbana: University of Illinois Press, 1973.

Benton, F. Warren, et al. *Prison and Jail Security.* Urbana, Ill.: National Clearinghouse for Criminal Justice Planning and Architecture, 1974.

Blank, Lucile E. "Education in a Short-Term Institution."*American Journal of Correction* 28, no. 6 (November–December 1966): 21–23.

Blumer, A. H. *Jail Management: A Course for Jail Administrators.* Washington, D.C.: U. S. Government Printing Office, 1970.

Blumer, A. H., ed. *Jail Operations.* Washington, D.C.: U.S. Government Printing Office, 1970. (Six booklets of a programmed instruction course.)

Boyd, B. A. "Our Jails and the Psychiatrist's Examination and Treatment of the Disturbed Offender." *Canadian Journal of Corrections* 6 (October 1964): 477–79.

Brent, W. S. "The National Jail Association, Inc." *American Journal of Correction* 27, no. 4 (July–August 1965): 43.

Bridenbaugh, Carl. *Cities in the Wilderness: Urban Life in America 1625–1742.* New York: Capricorn Books, 1964.

Brown, Emily Sophie. "The County Jail in Connecticut." *Journal of Criminal Law and Criminology* 17, no. 3 (November 1926): 369–374.

Burns, Henry. *Origins and Development of Jails in America,* Carbondale: Southern Illinois University Center for the Study of Crime, Delinquency and Corrections, 1971.

Burns, Henry. "The American Jail in Perspective." *Crime and Delinquency* 17, no. 4 (October 1971): 447–55.

Busher, Walter H. *Ordering Time to Serve Prisoners: A Manual for the Planning and Administration of Work Release.* Washington, D.C.: U.S. Department of Justice, n.d.

Cahn, William. "Report on the Nassau County Jail." *Crime and Delinquency* 19, no. 1 (January 1973): 1–14.

Caldwell, Robert G. *Criminology* 2nd ed. New York: Ronald Press, 1965. Chapters 20, 21 and 22.

California Board of Corrections. *A Study of California County Jails.* Sacramento: California Board of Corrections, 1970.

California Board of Corrections. *Jail Task Force Report.* Sacramento: California Board of Corrections, 1971.

California Board of Corrections. *Minimum Jail Standards.* Sacramento: California Board of Corrections, 1963.

Callahan, Joseph D. "New Programs at Chicago House of Correction." *American Journal of Correction* 26, no. 3 (May–June 1964): 6–8.

Carney, Louis P. *Introduction to Correctional Science.* New York: McGraw-Hill, 1974. Chapter 10.

Carpenter, Mary. *Our Convicts.* 1864. Reprint: Montclair, N.J.: Patterson Smith Publishing Corporation, 1969.

Carter, Robert M., et al. *Corrections in America.* New York: Lippincott, 1975. Chapter 5.

Case, John D. "Modern Corrections in an Old County Jail." *American Journal of Correction* 27, no. 1 (January–February 1965): 4–6, 8–9.

Casey, Roy. "Keeping People Out of Jail." *Proceedings of American Prison Association 1939.* Pp. 453–56.

Casey, Roy. "Missouri Jail Survey." *Proceedings of the Seventh Annual Congress of The American Prison Association.* Cincinnati, Ohio, October 1940.

Chambliss, William J., ed. *Crime and the Legal Process.* New York: McGraw-Hill, 1969.

Citizens' Task Force. *Report on Regional Community Treatment Centers for Women.* Philadelphia: Pennsylvania Program for Women and Girl Offenders, 1970.

Collins, Paul. "We Can do it for Ourselves." Paper presented to the Third Annual Washington State Jailers Association Conference, Spokane, Washington, 1976.

Committee on Standard Act for State Correction Services of the National Council on Crime and Delinquency and the American Correctional Association. "Standard Act for State Correctional Services." *Crime and Delinquency* 13, no. 3 (July 1967): 391–420.

Conrad, J. "Counties and the Correctional Crisis," *American County* 37, no. 10 (November 1972): 15–19.

Correctional Master Plan Summary, State of Hawaii. Urbana, Ill.: National Clearinghouse for Criminal Justice Planning and Architecture, 1973.

Coughlin, J. "Counties Can Lead Community-based Corrections." *American County* 37, no. 10 (November 1972): 13–14.

The County Jail. New York: The National Committee on Prisons and Prison Labor, 1929.

County and City Jails. Washington, D.C.: U.S. Department of Commerce, Bureau of the Census, 1933.

Crawford, William. *Report on the Penitentiaries of the United States.* 1835. Reprint: Montclair, N.J.: Patterson Smith, 1969.

Criminal Justice Monograph: Prevention of Violence in Correctional Institutions. Washington, D.C.: U.S. Department of Justice, 1973.

Criminal Justice Coordinating Council and Vera Institute of Justice. *In Lieu of Arrest—Manhattan Bowery Project: Treatment of Homeless Alcoholics.* New York: Criminal Justice Coordinating Council and Vera Institute of Justice, n.d.

Cromwell, Paul F. *Jails and Justice.* Springfield, Ill.: Charles C. Thomas, 1975.

Cross, William T. "Jails, Lockups and Police Stations." *Journal of Criminal Law and Criminology* 7, no. 3 (September 1916): 379–92.

Culbertson, R. G., and Magra, R. *Jail Evaluation, A Standards Report.* Lansing, Mich.: Michigan Council on Crime and Delinquency, 1975.

Dahlin, Donald C. *South Dakota Jails: Current Conditions and Proposed Directions.* Vermillion, S.D.: n.p., 1971.

Davis, Alan J. "Sexual Assaults in the Philadelphia Prison System and Sheriff's Van." *Trans-action* 6, no. 2 (December 1968): 8–16.

Davis, Jerome. *Report of the Legislative Commission on Jails With a Special Study on the Jail Population of Connecticut.* Hartford: State of Connecticut, 1934.

Dehlin, D. J., and Millan, V. D. *Jail Survey of City and County Law Enforcement Agencies.* Washington, D.C.: Law Enforcement Assistance Administration, 1969.

DeLacey, Kenneth. *Jail Inspection Report—1973 to the 43rd Legislature.* Olympia: State of Washington, 1974.

Deming, V., and Kilpack, R. *County Jail: A Handbook for Citizen Action.* Media, Penn.: Friends Suburban Project, 1973.

Design for Change: A Program for Correctional Management. Sacramento, Calif.: Institute of Crime and Delinquency, 1968.

DeVine, Russell B. *The American Jail: What It Is and What to Do About It.* New York: The American Prison Association, 1937.

DeVine, Russell B. "What Price Jails—A Critical Survey of a Depression Proof Industry." *Proceedings of the Sixty-Fifth Annual Congress of the American Prison Association,* October 1935. Pp. 302–13.

Dixon, L., and Davis, S. *City Jails: A Call to Action.* Washington, D.C.: Law Enforcement Assistance Administration, 1972.

Doleschal, Eugene. "Graduated Release." *Information Review on Crime and Delinquency.* December 1969, pp. 1–26.

Dowling, Oscar. "The Hygiene of Jails, Lock-ups and Police Stations." *Journal of Criminal Law and Criminology* 5, no. 5 (January 1915): 695–703.

Downey, John J. "Why Children Are in Jail and How to Keep Them Out," *Children* 17, no. 1 (January–February 1970): 21–26.

Driver, Robert W. "Municipal Justice Building—Orlando, Florida." *The Police Chief* 41, no. 1 (1974): 40–41.

Drucker, Paula K. "Short-Term Education in a Short-Term Penal Institution." *Crime and Delinquency* 12, no. 1 (January 1966): 58–69.

Dwoskin, Sidney I. "Jail as a Condition of Probation." *California Youth Authority* 15 (1962): 10.

Erwin, John R. "Cook County Jail's Short-term Educational Program." *American Journal of Correction* 32, no. 1 (January–February 1970): 14–18.

Fishman, Joseph F. *Crucibles of Crime.* New York: Cosmopolis Press, 1923.

Flynn, Edith E. "Jails and Criminal Justice." In *Prisoners in America,* edited by Lloyd E. Ohlin. Englewood Cliffs, N.J.: Prentice-Hall, 1973. Pp. 49–85.

Food Service in Jails. Washington, D.C.: The National Sheriff's Association, 1974.

Fox, Lionel W. *The English Prison and Borstal System.* London: Routledge and Kegan Paul, 1952.

Fox, Vernon. *Introduction to Corrections,* Englewood Cliffs, N.J.: Prentice-Hall, 1972. Chapter 4.

Friedman, Sidney, and Esselstyn, T. Conway. "The Adjustment of Children of Jail Inmates." *Federal Probation* 29, no. 4 (December 1965): 55–59.

Friel, C. M. "Jail Dilemma: Some Solutions." *American County* 37, no. 10 (November 1972): 9–11.

Gill, Howard B. "Correctional Philosophy and Architecture." *Journal of Criminal Law, Criminology and Police Science* 53, no. 3 (September 1962): 312–22.

Glaser, Daniel. "Some Notes on Urban Jails." In *Crime in the City,* edited by Daniel Glaser. New York: Harper and Row, 1970.

Goldfarb, Ronald. "No Room in the Jail." *New Republic* 154, no. 10 (March 5, 1966): 12–14.

Goldfarb, Ronald. *Jails: The Ultimate Ghetto of the Criminal Justice System.* Garden City, N.Y.: Doubleday, Anchor, 1975.

Governor's Citizens Committee on Delinquency and Crime. *Report of the Governor's Citizens Committee on Delinquency and Crime.* St. Louis: Office of the Governor, 1968.

Grunhut, Max. *Penal Reform.* New York: Clarendon Press, 1948.

Guidelines for Jail Operations, Washington, D.C.: The National Sheriffs' Association, 1972.

Handbook of Correctional Institution Design and Construction. Washington, D.C.: Federal Bureau of Prisons, 1949.

A Handbook on Jail Architecture. Washington, D.C.: The National Sheriffs' Association, 1975.

Hart, Hastings H. *Plans for City Police Jails and Village Lockups.* New York: Russell Sage Foundation, 1932.

Hart, Hastings H. "Police Jails and Village Lockups." In *Report on Penal Institutions, Probation and Parole, No. 9.* Washington D.C.: National Commission on Law Observance and Enforcement, 1931. Pp. 327–344.

Hartinger, Walter, et al. *Corrections: A Component of the Criminal Justice System.* Pacific Palisades, Calif.: Goodyear Publishing Co., 1973.

Henderson, Charles R., ed. *Penology and Reformatory Institutions.* New York: Charities Publication Committee, 1910. Chapter 2.

Hoffer, Frank William, Mann, Delbert M., and House, Floyd N. *The Jails of Virginia.* New York: D. Appleton-Century, 1933.

Howard, John. *The State of the Prisons in England and Wales.* London: privately printed, 1777.

Idaho Law Enforcement Planning Commission. *State of Idaho Jail Survey.* Boise: Idaho Law Enforcement Planning Commission, 1969.

Illinois Department of Corrections. *Illinois County Jail Standards.* Springfield: Illinois Department of Corrections, 1971.

Illinois Department of Corrections. *Municipal Jail and Lockup Standards.* Springfield: Illinois Department of Corrections, 1971.

Illinois State Charities Commission. *First Annual Report.* Springfield: Illinois State Journal Company, 1911.

Institute for the Study of Crime and Delinquency. *Model Community Correction Program: Appendix Report—The Model Misdemeanant Probation Program.* Sacramento: Institute for the Study of Crime and Delinquency, 1969.

Institute for the Study of Crime and Delinquency. *Model Community Correctional Program: Crime and Its Correction in San Joaquin County.* Sacramento: Institute for the Study of Crime and Delinquency, 1969.

Iowa Crime Commission. *Area Correctional Centers.* Des Moines: Iowa Crime Commission, 1972.

Ives, George. *A History of Penal Methods.* London: Stanley Paul and Company, 1914.

Jacobs, Ann, et al. *The Educational Program of the D.C. Jail: Analysis and Recommendations.* Washington, D.C.: District of Columbia Corrections Department, 1971.

Jail Security, Correspondence Course for Jailers. Vol. 2. Washington, D.C.: U.S. Bureau of Prisons, 1967.

John Howard Association. *Chicago Police Lock-ups,* Chicago: John Howard Association, 1963.

John Howard Association. *Consultation Report: Nueces County Jail—Corpus Christi, Texas.* Chicago: John Howard Association, 1972.

John Howard Association. *Summary of the Interim Report on the Cook County Jail.* Chicago: John Howard Association, 1967.

Johnson, Elmer H. *Crime, Correction and Society.* 3rd ed. Homewood, Ill.: Dorsey Press, 1974. (Chapter 15.)

Jordan, P. D. "The Close and Stinking Jail." In *Frontier Law and Order: Ten Essays.* Lincoln: University of Nebraska Press, 1970.

Kentucky Law Enforcement and Crime Commission. *Kentucky Jails.* Frankfort: Kentucky Law Enforcement and Crime Prevention Commission, 1969.

Ketterling, Marvin E. *Rehabilitation of Women in the Milwaukee County Jail: An Exploratory Experiment.* Ann Arbor: University of Michigan, 1965.

Kinsella, Nina. "The County Jails." *Proceedings of the American Prison Association, 1935.* Pp. 283-89.

Kirkpatrick, A. M. "Jails in Historical Perspective." *Canadian Journal of Corrections* 6 (October 1964): 405–18.

Korn, Richard R., and McCorkle, Lloyd W. *Criminology and Penology.* New York: Holt, Rinehart, and Winston, 1967. Chapter 16.

Lee, Sharron. *Comparisons and Considerations for Social Services in Local Jails.* Seattle, Wash.: Seattle-King County Corrections Development Project, 1972.

Leonard, E. M. *The Early History of English Poor Relief.* Cambridge: University Press, 1900.

Let's Look at the Jailer's Jobs. Correspondence Course for Jailers. Vol. 1 Washington, D.C.: U.S. Bureau of Prisons, 1967.

Lewis, Burdette G. "Our Lousy Jails." *Proceedings of the Sixty-Fifth Annual Congress of the American Prison Association,* October 1935. Pp. 290-295.

Lewis, O. F. *The Development of American Prisons and Prison Customs 1776-1845.* (Albany: The Prison Association of New York, 1922.) Reprint: Montclair, N.J.: Patterson Smith, 1967.

Lincke, Jack. "Town of Dover Law Enforcement Center." *The Police Chief* 41, no. 1 (January 1974): 43-44.

Loth, David. "The Westchester Misdemeanant Survey—A Sample of 'Nine-Tenths of All American Crime.'" *Crime and Delinquency* 13, no. 2 (April 1967): 330-36.

Loveland, Frank. *Correctional Institution and Services of Connecticut.* Philadelphia: American Foundation, 1966.

Lunden, Walter A. "The American Jail." *Police* 16, no. 6 (February 1972): 6-10.

MacCormick, Austin H. "Children in Our Jails." *The Annals* 261 (January 1949): 150-57.

McArthur, Virginia, et al. *Cost Analysis of the District of Columbia Work Release Program.* Washington, D.C.: District of Columbia Corrections Department, 1970.

McCord, Clinton P. "A Survey of the Albany County Jail and Penitentiary from Social, Physical and Psychiatric Viewpoints." *Journal of Criminal Law and Criminology* 15, no. 1 (May 1924): 42-67.

McCrea, Tully L. *Report of Adult Correctional Facilities Consultation, San Mateo County, California.* New York: National Council on Crime and Delinquency, 1970.

McCrea, Tully L. and Gottfredson, Don M. *A Guide to Improved Handling of Misdemeanant Offenders.* Washington, D.C.: U.S. Department of Justice, 1974.

McGee, Richard A. "Our Sick Jails." *Federal Probation* 31, no. 1 (1971): 3-8.

McKelvey, Blake. *American Prisons: A Study in American Social History Prior to 1915.* Chicago: University of Chicago Press, 1936.

McMillan, David. "Work Furlough for the Jailed Prisoner." *Federal Probation* 29, no. 1 (March 1965): 33-34.

McReynolds, K. L. "Physical Components of Correctional Goals." Master of Architecture thesis, Université de Montréal, 1970.

Mann, Charles, and Taedter, Carl. *The Jails of Missouri: A report for the Governor's Citizens Committee on Delinquency and Crime.* Jefferson City: State Printing Office, 1968.

Massachusetts Governor's Committee on Jails and Houses of Correction. *Report.* Boston: State Printing Office, 1965.

Mattick, Hans W. *A Unified City-County Department of Corrections for Chicago and Cook County.* Chicago: John Howard Association, 1960.

Mattick, Hans W. "The Contemporary Jails of the United States: An Unknown and Neglected Area of Justice." In *Handbook of Criminology,* edited by Daniel Glaser. Chicago: Rand McNally, 1974, Pp. 777-848.

Mattick, Hans W. *The Cook County Jail.* Chicago: Office of the Sheriff of Cook County, 1957.

Mattick, Hans W. and Aikman, Alexander B. "The Cloacal Region of American Corrections." *The Annals of the American Academy of Political and Social Science* 381 (January 1969): 109–118.

Mennel, Robert M. *Thorns and Thistles.* Hanover, N.H. The University Press of New England, 1973.

Mennerick, Lewis A. *The Impact of the External Environment on a County Jail School.* Ann Arbor: University of Michigan Press, 1972.

Menninger, Karl. *The Crime of Punishment.* New York: Viking Press, 1968.

Mimms, Thomas B. "Minimum Standards for the County Jail." *Proceedings of the Sixty-Fifth Annual Congress of the American Prison Association,* October 1935. Pp. 296–301.

Minnesota Corrections Department. *A Comprehensive Plan for Regional Jailing and Juvenile Detention in Minnesota.* St. Paul: Minnesota Corrections Department, 1971.

Mitchell, R. J., and Leys, M. D. R. *A History of London Life.* Baltimore: Penguin Books, 1958. Chapter 11.

Model Cities Agency. *Field Report: Jail Rehabilitation.* Lansing, Mich.: Model Cities Agency, 1971.

Model Cities Agency. *Field Report: Lucas County Jail Rehabilitation Services.* Toledo, Ohio: Model Cities Agency, 1971.

Morris, Joe Alex. *First Offender: A Voluntary Program for Youth in Trouble with the Law.* New York: Funk and Wagnalls, 1970.

Moyer, Frederick D. "Criminal Justice and Its Facilities: A Pattern for Change." *The American County* 37, no. 10 (November 1972): 22.

Moyer, Frederick D., and Flynn, Edith E., eds. *Correctional Environments.* Urbana: National Clearinghouse for Criminal Justice Planning and Architecture, 1971.

Moyer, Frederick D., et al. *Guidelines for the Planning and Design of Regional and Community Correctional Centers for Adults.* Urbana: University of Illinois, 1971.

Moyer, Frederick D., et al. *Prototype Design for Small Jail, Modular Construction.* Urbana: University of Illinois Press, 1971.

Moynahan, J. M. "Am I a Professional." *The Police Chief* 37, no. 2 (February 1970): 24.

Moynahan, J. M. *Corrections in the County-City Jail, Spokane, Washington.* Spokane, Washington: Rehabilitative Services Program, 1974.

Nagel, William G. *The New Red Barn: A Critical Look at The Modern American Prison.* New York: Walker and Company, 1973.

National Advisory Commission on Criminal Justice Standards and Goals. *Corrections.* Washington, D.C.: Government Printing Office, 1973.

National Association of Counties. "Jail Inmate Rehabilitation Program." *American County* 37, no. 10 (November 1972): 11–12.

National Council on Crime and Delinquency Board of Trustees. "Institutional Construction: A Policy Statement." *Crime and Delinquency* 18, no. 4 (October 1972): 331–34.

National Criminal Justice Information and Statistics Service. *Survey of Inmates of Local Jails 1972 Advanced Report.* Washington, D.C.: Government Printing Office, 1972.

National Criminal Justice Information and Statistics Service. *The Nation's Jails.* Washington D.C.: Government Printing Office, 1975.

National Jail Association. "Jail Standards Approved by the National Jail Association." *National Jail Forum* 6 (1965): 7–12.

National Jail Census, 1970. Washington, D.C.: Law Enforcement Assistance Administration, U.S. Department of Justice, 1971.

National Sheriffs' Association. *Inmates' Legal Rights.* Washington, D.C.: The National Sheriffs' Association, 1974.

National Sheriffs' Association. *Jail Administration.* Washington, D.C.: The National Sheriffs' Association, 1974.

National Sheriffs' Association. *Jail Architecture.* Washington, D.C.: The National Sheriffs' Association, 1975.

National Sheriffs' Association. *Jail Programs.* Washington, D.C.: The National Sheriffs' Association, 1974.

National Sheriffs' Association. *Jail Security, Classification and Discipline.* Washington, D.C.: The National Sheriffs' Association, 1974.

National Sheriffs' Association. *Manual of Jail Administration.* Washington, D.C.: The National Sheriffs' Association, 1970.

National Sheriffs' Association. *Sanitation in the Jails.* Washington, D.C.: The National Sheriffs' Association, 1974.

Neil, Thomas C. "Education in the Alachua County Jail." *Journal of Correctional Education* 22, (1970): 15.

Newman, Charles L., and Bialen, Thomas R. *Work Release: An Alternative in Correctional Handling.* University Park: Pennsylvania State University Press, 1968.

Newman, Charles L., et al. *Local Jails and Drug Treatment.* University Park: Pennsylvania State University Press, 1976.

Newman, Charles L.; Parsonage, W.; and Price, B. R. *Jails and Prisons.* University Park: Pennsylvania State University Press, 1969.

New York State Commission of Investigation. *County Jails and Penitentiaries in New York State.* Albany: State Printing Office, 1966.

New York City Correction Board. *Task Force on the Role of the Chaplain in the New York City Correctional Institutions.* New York: New York City Correction Board, 1972.

Nimmer, Raymond. *Two Million Unnecessary Arrests.* Chicago: American Bar Foundation, 1971.

North Carolina Jail Study Commission. *A Challenge to Excellence: Local Jails in North Carolina.* Raleigh: State Printing Office, 1969.

Northern California Service League. *Final Report of the San Francisco Rehabilitation Project for Offenders.* San Francisco: Northern California Service League, 1968.

Northern California Service League. *The County Jail Inmates as a Subject for Rehabilitation.* San Francisco: Northern California Service League, 1964.

O'Connor, Gerald D. "The Impact of Initial Detention Upon Male Delinquents." *Social Problems* 18, no. 2 (Fall 1970): 194–99.

Pappas, Nick. *The Jail: Its Operation and Management.* Washington, D.C.: U.S. Bureau of Prisons, 1970.

Partnow, Louis. "Detention and the Untried and Probation." *Prison Journal* 38, no. 1 (April 1958): 22–26.

Partnow, Louis. "Toward a Program for the Untried Adult in Detention." *Prison Journal* 37, no. 1 (April 1957): 12–46.

Paschal, Caraker. "Relation of Architecture to Correctional and Rehabilitative Facilities." *The Police Chief* 41, no.1 (January 1974): 50.

Pennsylvania General Assembly Joint State Government Commission. *The County Prisons and Jails of Pennsylvania.* Philadelphia: American Foundation, Institute of Corrections, 1965.

Platt, Anthony M. *The Child Savers.* Chicago: University of Chicago Press, 1969.

Poynton, Richard. "Adult Basic Education Behind Bars." *Extern Network of Adult Education Leaders Newsletter,* January 1972, pp 6–9.

Poynton, Richard. "Volunteers Contribute to Rehabilitation at Ingham County Jail," *Volunteer Administration,* September 1971.

President's Commission on Law Enforcement and Administration of Justice. *Task Force Report Corrections.* Washington, D.C.: U.S. Department of Justice, 1967.

Pugh, Ralph B. *Imprisonment in Medieval England.* Cambridge: University Press, 1968.

Queen, Stuart A. *The Passing of the County Jail.* Menasha, Wisc.: Banta, 1920.

Rankin, A. "The Effect of Pre-Trial Detention." *New York University Law Review* 39, no. 4 (1964): 641–55.

Receiving Prisoners, Correspondence Course for Jailers. Vol. 3. Washington, D.C.; U.S. Bureau of Prisons, 1966.

(The) Residential Center: Corrections In The Community. Washington, D.C.; U.S. Bureau of Prisons.

Richmond, Mark S. *Classification of Jail Prisoners.* Washington, D.C.; U.S. Bureau of Prisons, Department of Justice, 1971.

Richmond, Mark S. "The Jail Blight." *Crime and Delinquency* 11, no. 2 (April 1965): 132–41.

Richmond, Mark S., ed: *Prisoner Management and Control.* Washington, D.C.: U.S. Bureau of Prisons, 1969.

Richmond, Mark S., and Aderhold, George W. *New Roles for Jails.* Washington, D.C.: Department of Justice, 1969.

Rickless, Walter C. *The Crime Problem.* 5th ed. New York: Appleton Century Crofts, 1973. Chapter 16.

Robinson, Louis N. *Jails: Care and Treatment of Misdemeanant Prisoners in the United States.* Philadelphia: John C. Winston, 1944.

Robinson, Louis N. *Penology in the United States.* Philadelphia: John C. Winston, 1922. Chapter 3.

Robinson, Louis N. "The Perennial Jail Problem." *Journal of Criminal Law and Criminology* 35, no. 6 (March-April 1945): 369–74.

Robinson, Louis N. "The Relation of Jails to County and State." *Journal of the American Institute of Criminal Law and Criminology* 20, no. 3 (November 1929): 396–420.

Robinson, Louis N. "The Solution of the Jail Problem." *Journal of Criminal Law and Criminology* 6, no. 1 (May 1915): 101–3.

Root, Lawrence S. "Work Release Legislation." *Federal Probation* 36, no. 1 (March 1972): 38–42.

Rothman, David J. *The Discovery of the Asylum.* Boston: Little, Brown, 1971.

Rubin, Lillian. "The Racist Liberals—An Episode in a County Jail." *Trans-action* 5, no. 9 (September 1968): 39–44.

Rubington, Earl. "The Alcoholic and The Jail." *Federal Probation,* 29, no. 2 (June 1965): 30–33.

Rubington, Earl. "The Revolving Door 'Game'." *Crime and Delinquency* 12, no. 4 (October 1966): 332–38.

Rudoff, Alvin, et al. "Evaluating Work Furlough." *Federal Probation* 35, no. 1 (March 1971): 34–38.

Sandhu, Harjit S. "The Impact of Short-Term Institutionalisation on Prison Inmates." *British Journal of Criminology* 4, no. 3 (July 1964): 461–74.

Sarri, R. L. *Under Lock and Key.* Ann Arbor, Mich.: National Assessment of Juvenile Corrections, 1974.

Sheeter, R.; Newman, C. L.; and Case, J. "Systems Analysis of an Information System for a County Jail." *Law Enforcement Science and*

Technology II, ed. Cohen. Chicago: ITT Research Institute, 1968. Pp. 273–77.

Shurtleff, Caroline. *Annotated Bibliography on Jails.* Washington, D.C.: Department of Justice, Attorney General's Committee on Crime, about 1937.

Steiner, Jesse F., and Brown, Roy M. *The North Carolina Chain Gang.* Chapel Hill: The University of North Carolina Press, 1927.

Steinwald, Carolyn, et al. *Medical Care in U.S. Jails: A 1972 AMA Survey.* Chicago: American Medical Association, Center for Health Services Research and Development, 1973.

Stern, Leo. "Social Work Services in County Jails." *Proceedings of the Sixty-Fifth Annual Congress of the American Prison Association,* October 1935. Pp. 322–29.

A Study of California County Jails. Sacramento: California Board of Corrections, 1970.

A Study of County Jails in California. Sacramento: State Department of Correction, 1949.

Supervision of Prisoners, Correspondence Course for Jailers. Vol. 4. Washington, D.C.: U.S. Bureau of Prisons, 1966.

Teeters, Negley K. *The Cradle of the Penitentiary.* Philadelphia: The Pennsylvania Prison Society, 1955.

Teeters, Negley K. *They Were in Prison,* Philadelphia: John C. Winston, 1947.

Tracy, James A. "County Jails." In Clyde B. Vedder et al. *Criminology: A Book of Readings.* New York: Holt, Rinehart, and Winston, 1953. Pp. 589–94.

United States Bureau of Prisons. *Correspondence Course for Jailers.* Washington, D.C.: U.S. Department of Justice. n.d.

University of North Carolina Institute of Government. *A Preliminary Study on Jails in North Carolina.* Chapel Hill: Institute of Government, 1967.

University of Tennessee Record Extension Series, Division of University Extension, Department of Community Service. *County Jails in Tennessee* 3, no. 3 (May 1926). Knoxville: University of Tennessee Press.

Virginia Department of Welfare and Institutions. *Commitments to County and City Jails and City Jail Farms.* Richmond: Virginia Department of Welfare and Institutions, 1964.

Ward, A. LeRoy. "Before and After in Neptune, New Jersey." *The Police Chief* 41, no. 1 (January 1974): 48–49.

Washington Department of Institutions. *Jail Inspection Report—1968.* Olympia: Washington Department of Institutions, 1968.

Webb, Sidney, and Webb, Beatrice. *English Prisons Under Local Government.* New York: Longmans, Green and Company, 1922.

Wheeler, Ruth Dunlap. "The Problem of the County Jail." *Journal of Criminal Law and Criminology* 15, no. 4 (February 1925): 620–30.

Whiffen, Marcus. *The Public Buildings of Williamsburg.* Williamsburg, Va.: Colonial Williamsburg, 1958.

Whitman, John L. "Jails, Lockups and Police Stations." *Journal of Criminal Law and Criminology* 6, no. 2 (July 1915): 240–48.

Wice, Paul, and Simon, Rita James. "Pretrial Release: A Survey of Alternative Practices." *Federal Probation* 34, no. 4 (December 1970): 60–61.

Wines, E. C., and Dwight, Theodore W. *Report on the Prisons and Reformatories of the United States and Canada.* Albany, N.Y.: Van Benthuysen and Son's Steam Printing House, 1867.

Wines, Frederick H. *Punishment and Reformation.* New York: Thomas Y. Crowell Co., 1919.

Wright, Roberts J. "What! The County Jail Again?". *Federal Probation* 11, no. 3 (September 1947): 17–20.

Zimmerman, W. Carbys. "Modern Jail Architecture." *Journal of Criminal Law and Criminology* 6, no. 5 (January 1916): 717–23.

Index

Abbeville County (S.C.), 72
"Act for the suppression of Rogues
...etc." (1699), 31
Act of 1790 (Penn.), 35-36
Aiken County (S.C.), 72
Akron, Ohio, 130
Alabama, 89
Albany County (N.Y.) Jail, 64-65;
penitentiary, 64-65
American Revolution, reform forces
growing out of, 34-35
Arkansas, 89, 95
Assizes of Clarendon (1166), 13
Auburn (N.Y.) prison, 37-38; prison
system, 36, 38

Bamberg County (S.C.), 72
Barnes, James, 28
Barnstable (Mass.) Jail, 48
Beaufort County (S.C.), 72
Beccaria, Cesare, 34
Bentham, Jeremy, 23, 34
Biddle, William, 28
Blackstone, Sir William, 34
Book of Orders (1630-1631), 19
Boston Jail, 47
Boston Prison Discipline Society,
37, 38, 45, 52; report of 1834, 46-
49
Bot, defined, 11
Bradford, William, 34
Bridenbaugh, Carl, 27
Bridewells, 25; origins, 17-19
Bristol Newgate jail (England), 20

Calhoun County (S.C.), 72
California, 86, 88, 89, 90, 94, 95;
inmate population of, 85
Cambridge (Mass.) Jail, 48-49
Capital punishment, restriction of, 5

Cary, Henry, 28
Census, method of taking, 84
Chain gangs, 61
Charity boards, 65
Cherokee County (S.C.), 72
Chester County (S.C.), 72
Chesterfield County (S.C.), 72
Chicago, 131
Children, confinement of, 43-45.
See also Juveniles
Children's Aid Society of Boston,
44-45
Cities in the Wilderness
(Bridenbaugh), 27
Clarendon County (S.C.), 72
Clayton, William, 28
Clement XI (Pope), 34
Cleveland, 132; prison, 56
Colleton County (S.C.), 72-73
Comes stabuli, defined, 12-13
Common law, origins of, 14
Concord (Mass.) Jail, 49
Condorcet, Marquis de, 34
Connecticut, 84
Constables, 12-13
Cook, Rufus R., 45
Corporal punishment, decline of, 41
County jails, rules for inmates of,
185-86
County-city jail model, 100-101
Court decisions, 106-7
Court of Quarter Sessions
(England), 20
Criminal code, reform of, 35
Criminal justice system, changing
concepts, 1-2; colonial, 27, 33-34;
early Anglo-Saxon, 11; English
early modern, 17-24; medieval,
11-15
Criminology, origins of, 5-6

Danville (Ill.) Jail, 62
Darlington County (S.C.), 73
Debt, imprisonment for, 42-43
Dedham (Mass.) Jail and House of
  Correction, 47
Delaware, 4, 84
Diderot, Denis, 34
Dillon County (S.C.), 73
Disease epidemics, 22
District of Columbia, 86, 88, 89, 91,
  94; history of jails, 123-24
Dunking stool, 27
Dutch West India Company, 27-28
Dwight, Louis, 37, 45

Eastern Penitentiary (Cherry Hill,
  Philadelphia), 37
Edgartown (Mass.) Jail, 48
Education facilities, 88-89
Edward VII, 17
Elizabeth I, 20, 26
England, centralization of jails, 101;
  origins of jail system, 9-15
"Essay Towards the Reformation of
  Newgate and Other Prisons in
  and About London," 21

Fairfield County (S.C.), 73
Federal Bail Reform Act of 1966,
  86
Fee system, 30
Felons, confinement of, 107-8
Feudal justice, 11-12
First Annual Report of the Illinois
  State Charities Commission
  (1910), quoted, 65-66
Fishman, Joseph F., quoted, 72-74,
  80
Florida, 86, 88, 90; inmate popula-
  tion, 85
Franklin, Benjamin, 34

Gaol Act of 1823 (England), 23
"Gaol delivery" process, 14
Garofalo, Raffaele, 5-6
Georgetown County (S.C.), 73
Georgia, 70, 86, 88; inmate popula-
  tion of, 85

"Great Law" of 1682 (Penn.), 31
Greenfield (Mass.) Jail, 47
Grunhut, Max, quoted, 21

Hart, Hasting H., 83, 125n; quoted,
  74, 75
Hartford (Conn.) county jail, 52-55;
  New County Prison, 119-21
Haviland, John, 37
Hawaii, 88, 89
Henry II, 13, 14
Henry VIII, 17
House of correction, 25, 30, 31, 70;
  origins of, 17-18, 19
House of Refuge: Boston, 44; New
  York City, 44
Howard, John, 21-22, 34
Hume, David, 34

Idaho, 89, 94, 95
Illinois, 86, 95
Illinois State Charities Commission,
  First Annual Report, quoted, 65-
  66
Indiana, 86
Industries, jail, 108
Inmates, abnormal behavior, 153-
  54; classification system, 111;
  numbers of, 85; rules for
  guidance, 185-86; types of reten-
  tion, 86-88

Jail administrators, 99-100
Jail fever (typhus), 22
Jail Managers Association, 76
Jailers, 76-78; associations, 76;
  codes of ethics, 112-13; professionalism, 97-98; recruitment and
  training, 98-99; wages, 111-12
Jails: abnormal behavior of inmates,
  153-55; alternatives to confinement, 102-3; architecture, 99;
  census of U.S., 83-95, 167-83;
  changing functions, 80-81; classes
  of inmates, 103-4; classification of
  inmates, 111; in colonial
  America, 25-32; community interest, 103; confinement of felons,

107; confinement practices, 36; contemporary, 67-82; county-city model, 100-101; defined, 4; District of Columbia, 123-24; English early modern, 17-24; expenditures and planned construction, 94-95; financing, 71; frontier, 61-62; functions in medieval England, 13-15; general research on, 105-6; general statistics on, 85; high-rise, 79-80; impact of court decisions on, 106-7; industries, 108-9; juvenile population in, 85-86; lack of adaptation, 2; Massachusetts, 46-49; Minnesota law of 1895, 67-69; nature of facilities, 88-90; nineteenth century changes, 41-66; nomenclature of personnel, 112; number of employees, 94-95; Ohio, 55-60; operating jursidiction, 10; overcrowding, 91-94; Pennsylvania system, 37; prisons different from, 2-4, 10; public committees, 106; reform movements, 5, 20-24, 34-39; regional/state control, 101; retention authority, 94; return rate, 80-81; role of, 102; rules, 108-9; rules for inmates, 185-86; safety and sanitation, 104-5; separation of sexes/races, 64; ship hulks used as, 23-24; South Carolina, 72-74; standards, 141-52; studies of treatment, 105; treatment programs, 81, 108, 154-55; twentieth century problems, 78-79; type of retention, 86-88; types of security, 110-11; volunteer workers, 109-10

Juveniles, and crime, 45; in adult institutions, 85-86; type of retention, 86-88

Kentucky, 89, 90
King's Bench jail (England), 20
Korn, Richard R., 13

Lancaster County (S.C.), 73
Lane, E., quoted, 55-60
Laurens County (S.C.), 73
Lenox (Mass.) Jail, 46
Leonard, E. M., quoted, 20
Lexington County (S.C.), 73
Lockups, 71-72, 125-40
Los Angeles, 131
Louisiana, 9
Lownes, Caleb, 34

McCorkle, Lloyd W., 13
Maine, 89, 90, 94
Marion County (S.C.), 73
Marlboro County (S.C.), 74
Marshalsea jail (England), 20
Maryland, 90, 91, 95
Massachusetts, 70, 86, 89, 90; summary of laws (1830), 42-43
Massachusetts Bay Colony, 31
Maximum security jail, 110
Medical facilities, 89, 90
Medium security jails, 110
Michigan, 88
Millbank penitentiary (England), 23
Minimum security jails, 110
Miniprison concept, 101
Minnesota, 127, 133; General Laws of 1895, quoted, 67-69; State Board of Corrections and Charities, 68, 69
Mississippi, 89, 94, 95
Missouri, 89
Montana, 90
Montesquieu, Baron de, 34
Morning Review (Spokane), quoted, 63
Mulrooney, Edward P., 131

Nantucket (Mass.) Jail, 48
National Commission on Law Observance and Enforcement, 130
National Criminal Justice Information and Statistics Service, 83
National Jail Census 1970, 84; statistics, 167-83

National Jail Managers Association, 97
National Jailers Association, 76, 97
National Sheriffs' Association, 75; jail standards, 141-52
Nevada, 89
New Amsterdam, 27-28
New Bedford (Mass.) Jail and House of Correction, 48
New County Prison (Hartford), 119-21
New England, 126
New Hampshire, 88, 90, 94
New Jersey, 89, 91, 95, 127
New Plymouth Colony, 31
New York City, 28-29, 130, 131, 132; Adolescent Remand Center, 85; Reformatory, 85
New York State, 86, 88, 89, 91, 94, 95, 127, 133; inmate population, 85
New York State Commission of Correction, 127
Newgate Prison (Simsbury, Conn.), 35
Newport, R.I., 27
Norfolk jail (England), 20
North Carolina, 41
North Central region, inmate population, 85; jail facilities, 90; overcrowding, 91; type of retention, 86-87
North Dakota, 95
Northampton (Mass.) Jail, 46
Northeast, inmate population, 85; number of jails, 89, 90; overcrowding, 91; type of retention, 86-87

Ohio, 86, 88; survey of jails, 55-60
Oklahoma, 127
Omaha, Neb., 131
Overcrowding, 91-94

Paine, Thomas, 34
Peel, Sir Robert, 23
Penn, William, 31, 34

Pennsylvania, 31, 32, 36-37, 38, 86, 88, 90, 95, 126; inmate population, 85; jail system, 37
Pennsylvania Assembly, 28
Pennsylvania Department of Welfare, 127
Philadelphia, 28, 130, 132; House of Refuge, 44
Philadelphia Society for Alleviating the Miseries of Public Prison, 35, 36, 38
Pillory, 26
Plymouth (Mass.) Jail, 98
Police jails, 125-40
Portsmouth, R.I., 27
Prison riot, first U.S., 35
Prison system, origin of modern concept, 35-36
Prisoners, life in early modern period, 20
Prisons, American development of, 33; different from jails, 2-4, 10; post-Revolutionary, 35-39
Protestant Episcopal church, 35
Public jail committees, 106
Punishments: colonial, 26-27; medieval, 14-15; reform of, 35

Quakers, 34, 35

Recreational facilities, 88
Reeve, defined, 12
Reform movements, 5, 34-39; English, 20-24
Reform schools, 44, 45
Regionalization of control, 101
Retention authority, 94
Rhode Island, 4, 84
Robinson, Louis N., quoted, 13, 31
Rogers, Thomas, 48
Romilly, Sir Samuel, 34
"Rotary jail," 64
Rush, Benjamin, 34

St. Louis, 131
Sanborn, Franklin B., quoted, 45
Sentencing practices, 107
"Separate system," 37

Sheriffs, 70, 100; origins, 12
Ship hulk jails, 23-24
Simsbury, Conn., 35
Smith, Adam, 34
Smith, Alfred, quoted, 52-53
Society for Promoting Christian Knowledge, 21
South, the: inmate population of, 85; jail facilities of, 90; overcrowding of jails, 91
South Boston House of Correction, 47, 50-52
South Carolina, 88, 95; jails, 72-74
South Dakota, 95
Southwest, Spanish legal influences in, 9
Spokane (Wash.) Jail, 63
Springfield (Mass.) Jail, 46
"Squirrel cage," 64
Stadt Huys City Hall (New Amsterdam), 28
State administration of jail, 4, 101
Statute of Westminster (1275), 13
Stockades, 70
Stocks, 26
Strickland, William, 37
Suffolk County Court (Mass.), 28

Taunton (Mass.) Jail, 47-48
Tennessee, 89
Texas, 86, 88, 94; inmate population, 85
Third degree, 127
Tithing system, 12
Transport of prisoners, 23
Treatment programs, 81, 109, 154-55
Turgot, Anne Robert Jacques, 34
Turnkey fee, 70
Typhus epidemics, 22

U.S. Bureau of the Census, 84, 125
Urbanism and the rise of jails, 9-10

Vagabonds, late medieval, 17
Vaux, Richard, 34
Vaux, Robert, 34
Vermont, 89, 90; inmate population, 85
Vicecomes, defined, 13
Virginia, 89, 90
Visiting facilities, 89
Vollmer, August, 132
Voltaire, Francois Marie Arouet de, 34
Volunteer workers, 109-10

Walnut Street Jail (Penn.), 35-36
Warren, Joel, 63
Washington, 95
Washington State Criminal Justice Training Commission, course for jailers, 76-78
Washington State Jailers Association, constitution, 157-66
Wergild, defined, 11
West, jail facilities, 90; overcrowding, 91; type of retention, 86
West Virginia, 95
Westborough (Mass.) reform school, 44
Western Penitentiary (Pittsburgh), 37
Westward movement, 61-62
Wethersfield, Conn., 35
Whipping posts, 26-27
White, George, 20
White, William, 34, 35
Wickersham, George W., 130
William the Conqueror, 12
Williamsburg, Va., 29-30
Wisconsin, 90, 95
Wite, define, 11
Worcester (Mass.) House of Correction, 47; Jail, 47
Workhouses, 19, 25, 30-31, 70